WORLD P
AN ABBEY THEAT

G000065736

ABBEY THEATRE
SHUSH
ELAINE MURPHY

Premiered by the Abbey Theatre
on the Abbey stage on 12 June 2013.

The Abbey Theatre gratefully acknowledges
the financial support of the Arts Council of
Ireland and the support of the Department
of the Arts, Heritage and the Gaeltacht.

Abbey Theatre **12 June 2013**
Civic Theatre **23 July 2013**
Pavilion Theatre **30 July 2013**

CAST (IN ORDER OF APPEARANCE)

Breda	Deirdre Donnelly
Marie	Barbara Brennan
Irene	Ruth Hegarty
Clare	Eva Bartley
Ursula	Niamh Daly

Director	Jim Culleton
Set Design	Anthony Lamble
Lighting Design	Kevin McFadden
Costume Design	Niamh Lunny
Sound Design	Denis Clohessy
Movement Co-ordinator	Liz Roche
Voice Director	Andrea Ainsworth
Company Stage Manger	Tara Furlong
Deputy Stage Manger	Anne Kyle
Assistant Stage Manger	Orla Burke
Casting Director	Kelly Phelan
Hair and Make-Up	Val Sherlock
Graphic Design	Zero-G
Set Construction	Theatre Production Services Ltd.
Scenic Artist	Sandra Butler
Special Effects	Craig Starkie and Se Purcell
Sign Language Interpreter	Vanessa O'Connell
Audio Description	Brid Ní Ghruagáin
	Maureen Portsmouth
Captioning	Paula Carraher
	Ruth McCreery

Audio described and captioned performances are provided by Arts and Disability Ireland with funding from the Arts Council of Ireland.

WORLD PREMIERE
AN ABBEY THEATRE COMMISSION

ABBEY THEATRE

SHUSH

ELAINE MURPHY

Shush by Elaine Murphy is an Abbey Theatre commission.

Shush is part of our published playscript series.
For further titles in the series please visit
www.abbeytheatre.ie

SPECIAL THANKS TO

*Amanda Coogan, Paula Furlong, Elayne Power, Dublin Simon Community and
Kathy Smyth from Butlers Chocolates for their kind donation of chocolates.*

accenture
High performance. Delivered.

Please note that the text of the play which appears in this
volume may be changed during the rehearsal process and
appear in a slightly altered form in performance.

ABBEY THEATRE AMHARCLANN NA MAINISTREACH

THE ABBEY THEATRE is Ireland's national theatre. It was founded by W.B. Yeats and Lady Augusta Gregory. Since it first opened its doors in 1904 the theatre has played a vital and often controversial role in the literary, social and cultural life of Ireland.

In 1905 the Abbey Theatre first toured internationally and continues to be an ambassador for Irish arts and culture worldwide.

The Abbey produces an annual programme of diverse, engaging, innovative Irish and international theatre and invests in and promotes new Irish writers and artists.

We do this by placing the writer and theatre-maker at the heart of all that we do, commissioning and producing exciting new work and creating discourse and debate on the political, cultural and social issues of the day. Our aim is to present great theatre art in a national context so that the stories told on stage have a resonance with artists and audiences alike.

Over the years, the Abbey Theatre has nurtured and premiered the work of major playwrights such as J.M. Synge and Sean O'Casey as well as contemporary classics from the likes of Sebastian Barry, Marina Carr, Bernard Farrell, Brian Friel, Frank McGuinness, Thomas Kilroy, Tom MacIntyre, Tom Murphy, Mark O'Rowe, Billy Roche and Sam Shepard.

We support a new generation of Irish writers at the Abbey Theatre including Richard Dormer, Gary Duggan, Stacey Gregg, Nancy Harris, Elaine Murphy and Carmel Winters.

None of this can happen without our audiences and our supporters. Annie Horniman provided crucial financial support to the Abbey in its first years. Many others have followed her lead by investing in and supporting our work.

IS Í AMHARCLANN NA MAINISTREACH amharclann náisiúnta na hÉireann. W.B. Yeats agus an Bantiarna Augusta Gregory a bhunaigh í. Riamh anall ón uair a osclaíodh a doirse i 1904, ghlac an amharclann ról an-tábhachtach agus, go minic, ról a bhí sách conspóideach, i saol liteartha, sóisialta agus cultúrtha na hÉireann.

I 1905 is ea a chuaigh complacht Amharclann na Mainistreach ar camchuairt idirnáisiúnta den chéad uair agus leanann sí i gcónaí de bheith ina hambasadóir ar fud an domhain d'ealaíona agus cultúr na hÉireann.

Léiríonn Amharclann na Mainistreach clár amharclannaíochta Éireannach agus idirnáisiúnta in aghaidh na bliana atá ilghnéitheach, tarraingteach agus nuálach agus agus infheistíonn sí a cuid acmhainní i scríbhneoirí agus ealaíontóirí nua de chuid na hÉireann agus cuireann sí chun cinn iad.

Déanaimid é sin tríd an scríbhneoir agus an t-amharclannóir a chur i gcroílár an uile ní a dhéanaimid, trí shaothar nua spreagúil a choimisiúnú agus a léiriú agus trí dhioscúrsa agus díospóireacht a chruthú i dtaobh cheisteanna polaitiúla, cultúrtha agus sóisialta na linne. Is í an aidhm atá againn ealaín amharclannaíochta den scoth a láithriú i gcomhthéacs náisiúnta ionas go mbeidh dáimh ag lucht ealaíne agus lucht féachana araon leis na scéalta a bhíonn á n-aithris ar an stáitse.

In imeacht na mblianta, rinne Amharclann na Mainistreach saothar mórdhrámadóirí ar nós J.M. Synge agus Sean O'Casey a chothú agus a chéadléiriú, mar a rinne sí freisin i gcás clasaicí comhaimseartha ó dhrámadóirí amhail Sebastian Barry, Marina Carr, Bernard Farrell, Brian Friel, Frank McGuinness, Thomas Kilroy, Tom MacIntyre, Tom Murphy, Mark O'Rowe, Billy Roche agus Sam Shepard.

Tugaimid tacaíocht don ghlúin nua Scríbhneoirí Éireannacha in Amharclann na Mainistreach, lena n-áirítear Richard Dormer, Gary Duggan, Stacey Gregg, Nancy Harris, Elaine Murphy agus Carmel Winters.

Ní féidir aon ní den chineál sin a thabhairt i gcrích gan ár lucht féachana agus ár lucht tacaíochta. Sholáthair Annie Horniman tacaíocht airgid ríthábhachtach don Mhainistir siar i mblianta tosaigh na hamharclainne. Lean iliomad daoine eile an dea-shampla ceannródaíochta sin uaithi ó shin trí infheistíocht a dhéanamh inár gcuid oibre agus tacaíocht a thabhairt dúinn.

Writer
Cast &
Creative
Team

ELAINE MURPHY

WRITER

ELAINE'S WORK AT the Abbey Theatre includes *Ribbons*, which was originally presented as part of the *The Fairer Sex* short play commission reading series and was staged as a Double Bill in the Peacock Theatre in February 2013. Her first play *Little Gem* premiered at the Dublin Fringe Festival in 2008. It won the Best Actress and The Fishamble New Writing Award before transferring to Edinburgh's Traverse Theatre during the Fringe Festival where it received the Carol Tambor Best of Edinburgh Award in 2009. *Little Gem* also visited the Peacock Theatre and was nominated for Best New Play and Best Actress at the Irish Times Theatre Awards. Elaine has received The Stewart Parker Award for Drama, a Zebbie for Best Theatre Script from the Irish Playwright and Screenwriters Guild and in 2011 was chosen as a participant of Six in the Attic, an Irish Theatre Institute Resource Sharing Initiative.

Elaine would like to take this opportunity to thank the cast and crew of *Shush*, Jim Culleton, Fiach Mac Conghail, literary 'midwife' Aideen Howard for her support and encouragement shown throughout the many drafts of this play, all the staff and its supporters at the Abbey Theatre, Claire, Jane and Siobhan at the Irish Theatre Institute, Amy Conroy and everyone at 'Six in the Attic', Graham Whybrow of the Stewart Parker Trust and finally for the love and support of her friends and family, especially Gavin 'The Saint' McCaffrey.

DEIRDRE DONNELLY

BREDA

DEIRDRE'S PREVIOUS WORK at the Abbey Theatre includes *Bookworms* (2012 and 2010), *An Ideal Husband, The Big House, The Crucible, Seven Jewish Children, A Month in the Country, Da, She Stoops to Folly, Drama at Inish, Too Late for Logic, You Can't Take It With You, Not I, All My Sons, Scenes from an Album, The Blue Macushla, The Well of Saints, Catchpenny Twist, Tarry Flynn, The Vicar of Wakefield, Twelfth Night, The Gathering, The Scatterin', Blood Wedding, The Whiteheaded Boy* and *In the Shadow of the Glen*. Other theatre work includes *Bedroom Farce, A Woman of No Importance, Little Women, Jane Eyre, Death of a Salesman, Les Liaisons Dangereuses, Aristocrats, Blithe Spirit* and *Agnes of God* (Gate Theatre), *The Scythe and the Sunset, Bedtime Story, Talk to Me Like the Rain, Old Times, She Stoops to Conquer, The J. Arthur Maginnis Story, As You Like It* and *Thieves Carnival* (Irish Theatre Company), *A Dream of Autumn*, Irish Times Theatre Award nomination for Best Supporting Actress 2005 and *Down Onto Blue* (Rough Magic Theatre Company), *Boesman and Lena* (Field Day Theatre Company), *Play it Again, Sam, Crooked in a Car-Seat* and *Private Lives* (Gemini), *Chapter Two* (Olympia Theatre), *A Delicate Balance* (Focus Theatre), *Nuts and Bolts*, one-woman play (Bewley's Café Theatre and Viking Theatre), *Over the River and Through the Woods* (Andrew's Lane Theatre) and *There Came A Gypsy Riding* (Livin' Dred). Film and television work includes *Quirke* (Element Pictures/ BBC), *Homemade* (ParkFilms), *Amber* (Amber Film Productions), *Cracks* (Scott-Free Productions), six seasons of *Ballykissangel* (World Productions/BBC), *Legend* (Icebox Productions/RTÉ), *The Irish RM* (Channel 4/RTÉ), *The Clinic* (Parallel Productions/RTÉ), *Fair City, Molloy, Thou Shalt Not Kill, Miracles and Miss Langan, The Last of the Summer* and *The Riordans* (RTÉ), *Fatal Lovers* (Lapaca Films), *The Fantasist* (ITC Films), *Attracta* and *Criminal Conversation* (BAC Films) and *Runway One* (BBC). Radio dramas include *Down Onto Blue, A Grand Reunion, Gentleman and Players, The Burning of Bridget Cleary, No Hate Going to Loss, Nomads, The Fishmonger's Wife, Border Crossing, Moving-In Day, The Intimacy Incentive, The House on Shareni Street, Oblivion* and *The Disappeared* (RTÉ), *Autumn Sunshine, Rotunda Blue, Say No to Shantonagh* and *The Hill Bachelors* (BBC).

BARBARA BRENNAN

MARIE

BARBARA'S PREVIOUS WORK at the Abbey Theatre includes *Big Love, Woman and Scarecrow, Lovers at Versailles, Down the Line, A Life, The Colleen Bawn, Kevin's Bed, A Picture of Paradise, The Importance of Being Earnest, A Woman of No Importance, She Stoops to Folly, Six Characters in Search of an Author, The Hostage, Angels in America, The Lilly Lally Show, Chamber Music, The Iceman Cometh, Drama at Inish, One Last White Horse* and *The Glass Menagerie.* Other theatre work includes *The Heiress,* Winner Irish Theatre Award for Best Actress 1979, *A Streetcar Named Desire,* Winner Irish Theatre Award for Best Supporting Actress 1981, *Hedda Gabbler,* Irish Theatre Award nomination for Best Actress 1984, *Salome, A Christmas Carol, Pygmalion, The Eccentricities of a Nightingale, Pride and Prejudice, The Beckett Festival, Festen, The Deep Blue Sea, Jane Eyre, Hayfever, Present Laughter* and *All My Sons* (Gate Theatre), *Cabaret* (Olympia Theatre) *By the Bog of Cats* (Wyndams Theatre, London), *Honour* (b*spoke Theatre Company), *Sleeping Beauty* and *Alice in Wonderland* (Landmark Productions), *Macbeth* and *The Making of 'Tis Pity She's a Whore* (Siren Productions) and *Steel Magnolias*

(Gaiety Theatre and National Tour). Film and television work includes *The Clinic, No Tears* and *Hell for Leather* (RTÉ), *Veronica Guerin* (Merrion Film Productions) and *The Tudors* (Showtime Productions).

RUTH HEGARTY

IRENE

RUTH'S PREVIOUS WORK at the Abbey Theatre includes *Tarry Flynn* and *Hotel Casanova.* Other theatre work includes *The Silver Tassie* (Druid), *Black Milk* (Prime Cut Productions), *Solemn Mass for a Full Moon in Summer, Is This About Sex?, Attempts on Her Life* and *Midden* (Rough Magic Theatre Company), *Unravelling the Ribbon* (Gúna Nua), *The Happy Ape* (Corcadorca), *Buddhist of Castleknock* (Fishamble: The New Play Company), *Women on the Verge, Brighton Beach Memoirs* and *The Odd Couple* (Andrew's Lane Theatre), *Mother Courage* and *Juno and the Paycock* (Royal Lyceum Theatre, Edinburgh), *Mackerel Sky* (Bush Theatre, London), *Communication Cord* (Field Day Theatre Company), *The Plough and the Stars* (Second Age Theatre Company), *The Cavalcaders* (Theatre Clwyd), *Ghosts* (Project Arts Centre), *The Mayor of Casterbridge* (Gaiety Theatre), *Educating Rita* (Gate Theatre) and *Big Maggie* and *The*

Informer (Olympia Theatre). Film and television work includes *Love/Hate, The Last Furlong, Whistleblower, Strumpet City, Caught in a Free State* and *Glenroe* (RTÉ), *War of the Buttons* (Enigma Productions), *Swansong: The Story of Occi Byrne* (Zanzibar Films), *Little Foxes* (Cineart Productions) and *Foreign Bodies* (BBC).

EVA BARTLEY
CLARE

EVA'S PREVIOUS WORK at the Abbey Theatre includes *The Last Days of a Reluctant Tyrant*. Other theatre work includes *Richard III* (Fast + Loose), *Hamlet* (Hong Kong Academy for Performing Arts), *The Merchant of Venice* (Second Age Theatre Company), *All's Well that Ends Well* (The Helix), *Harry in the Moonlight, Dancing at Lughnasa, Romeo and Juliet* and *The Night Garden* (Exeter Northcott Theatre), *Time Flies* and *Giants Have Us In Their Books* (X-Bel-Air), *Mixing it on the Mountain* (Calypso), *The Song from the Sea* and *Kevin's Story* (Barnstorm) and *A Christmas Carol* (Gate Theatre). Television work includes *Titanic: Blood and Steel* (Antena 3 Films), *Trial and Retribution* (ITV), *The Clinic* and *On Home Ground* (RTÉ). Eva is also a member of the comedy troupe The Brown Bread Players.

NIAMH DALY
URSULA

THIS IS NIAMH'S debut at the Abbey Theatre. Other theatre work includes *Lizzie Lavelle and the Vanishing of Emlyclough* and *Dr Ledbetter's Experiment* (Performance Corporation), *Jane Eyre* and *Pride and Prejudice* (Gate Theatre), *Alice in Wonderland* (The Helix), *Macbeth* (Second Age Theatre Company), *Rutherford and Son* and *The Secret Rapture* (Salisbury Playhouse), *Much Ado About Nothing* (Manchester Royal Exchange), *Dancing at Lughnasa* and *The Daughter in Law* (Bolton Octagon), *The Turn of the Screw* (Young Vic Theatre) and *The Snow Queen* (Dukes, Lancaster). Film and television work includes *Roy* (CBBC), *Camera Café* (Great Western Films), *The Cassidy's* (Graph Productions), *The Clinic* (RTÉ), *Coronation Street* (Granada Television), *Heartbeat* (ITV Productions) and *Midsomer Murders* (Bentley Productions). Niamh has also recorded the audio books for four of Marian Keyes' novels as well as working extensively in radio for RTÉ and BBC. Niamh trained at Manchester Met School of Theatre.

JIM CULLETON
DIRECTOR

JIM'S PREVIOUS WORK at the Abbey Theatre includes *Bookworms* by Bernard Farrell (2012 and 2010),

Standing up the Script in collaboration with Fighting Words, a reading of *Deirdre of the Sorrows* as part of Dublin: One City, One Book and *Yeats in his own Words* (Dublin, Sligo and Boston). The Abbey Theatre and Fishamble: The New Play Company collaborated on *Silent* in 2012 (Pat Kinevane) and *The Music of Ghost Light* in 2011 (Joseph O'Connor). Jim is the Artistic Director of Fishamble: The New Play Company for which he recently directed *Tiny Plays for Ireland* and *Tiny Plays for Ireland 2* by 50 writers, *Silent* (in over 30 Irish venues, European and Australian tours, New York, Los Angeles, winner of Fringe First, Herald Angel and Argus Angel awards), the multi award-winning *The Pride of Parnell Street* (Sebastian Barry) in London, New Haven, Paris, Wiesbaden, New York and Irish tours, *Turning Point* (Arts & Disability Ireland) in Dublin and Washington DC, the multi award-winning *Noah and the Tower Flower* (Sean McLoughlin) in Dublin, Bulgaria, Romania and New York and *Forgotten* (Pat Kinevane), on tour to over 40 Irish venues, 8 European countries, New York, Boston, Washington DC and Los Angeles. He has also directed for Woodpecker/Gaiety, 7:84 (Scotland), Project Arts Centre, Amharclann de hIde, Amnesty International, Tinderbox, The Passion Machine, The Ark, Second Age, RTÉ

Radio 1, The Belgrade, Semper Fi, TNL Canada, Scotland's Ensemble at Dundee Rep, Draíocht, Barnstorm, Roundabout, Trinity College Dublin School of Drama, Gúna Nua, Frontline Defenders, the Irish Council for Bioethics, Origin (New York) and RTÉ Lyric FM. He recently directed *Voices from the Frontline* starring Martin Sheen. Current projects for Fishamble include a range of Training, Development and Mentoring schemes and he will next direct *The Bruising of Clouds* by Sean McLoughlin. Jim has taught for New York University and University of Notre Dame, he is Adjunct Lecturer in the Trinity College Dublin School of Drama, he teaches a directing module for NUI Maynooth/Gaiety School of Acting, and in University College Dublin as part of Fishamble's Theatre Company-in-Association status with the college.

ANTHONY LAMBLE

SET DESIGN

ANTHONY'S PREVIOUS WORK at the Abbey Theatre includes the sets for *The Passing, The East Pier, Bookworms, The Comedy Of Errors* and the set for *The Playboy of the Western World*. Other design work includes *The Artist Man and Mother Woman* and *The Arthur Conan Doyle Appreciation Society* (Traverse Theatre, Edinburgh), *Third Finger,*

Left Hand (Trafalgar Studios), *The Two Worlds of Charlie F* (Bravo 22 Company at The Theatre Royal Haymarket), *BBC Comedy Sitcom Festival* (2011 and 2012), *Shivered* (Southwark Playhouse), *Much Ado About Nothing* and *Twelfth Night* (Ludlow Festival), *Relatively Speaking* (Watermill Theatre), *The Complaint* (Hampstead Studio), *For Once* (Pentabus Theatre tour), *Comedians* (Lyric Hammersmith), *Loot* (Tricycle), *Romeo and Juliet* (Globe/tour), *The English Game* (Headlong), *The Entertainer* (Old Vic), *Someone Who'll Watch Over Me* (West End), *The Price* (West End/Tricycle/tour), *The Caucasian Chalk Circle, Translations,* the premiere of *Sing Yer Heart Out for the Lads, A Midsummer Night's Dream* and *As You Like It* (National Theatre, London), *Measure For Measure, Richard III, The Roman Actor* and *King Baby* (Royal Shakespeare Company), *The World's Biggest Diamond, Incomplete and Random Acts of Kindness, Mother Teresa is Dead* and *Herons* (Royal Court Theatre), *The Common Pursuit, All Mouth* and *Breakfast With Jonny Wilkinson* (Menier Chocolate Factory), *Everything is Illuminated* (Hampstead), *Cleansed, Home, Sergeant Musgrave's Dance, Singer, Comedians, The Contractor* and *Troilus and Cressida* (Oxford Stage Company), *A Christmas Carol, In Celebration, Aristocrats, Spell of Cold Weather, The Sea, School of Night, Insignificance, The King of Prussia* and *Retreat From Moscow* (Chichester Festival Theatre), *Rum and Coca Cola* (also English Touring Theatre tour), *Bedroom Farce, Lettuce and Lovage, Exquisite Sister* and *Burning Everest* (West Yorkshire Playhouse), *Macbeth* (Dundee Rep), *Card Boys, All Of You Mine, Mortal Ash, Pond Life* and *Not Fade Away* (Bush Theatre). He has also designed shows for Sheffield Crucible, ETO, Shared Experience, Coventry Belgrade, Theatre Royal Northampton and Leicester Haymarket as well as the film, *The Secret Audience.* Dance and Opera credits include *Facing Viv* (English National Ballet), *L'Orfeo* (Opera City Tokyo), *Palace in The Sky* (English National Opera) and *Broken Fiction* (Royal Opera House).

NIAMH LUNNY
COSTUME DESIGN

NIAMH IS HEAD of the Costume Department at the Abbey Theatre. Her design work at the Abbey Theatre includes *The House, The East Pier, The Passing, Arrah-na-Pogue, The Seafarer, Only an Apple, Blue/Orange, Homelands, Portia Coughlan* and *I Do Not Like Thee Doctor Fell.*

Other work includes *Digging for Fire* (Rough Magic Theatre Company), *Tiny Plays for Ireland 1 and 2*, *The End of the Road* and *Shorts* (Fishamble: The New Play Company), *The Boys of Foley Street, Laundry* (ANU productions), *Swampoodle* (performed in Washington DC as part of Imagine Ireland), *Slattery's Sago Saga, The Seven Deadly Sins* and the short film *A Life* (The Performance Corporation), *Beware of the Story Book Wolves*, nominated for Best Costume Design Irish Times Theatre Awards (The Ark), *Operation Easter* (Calypso), *Here Lies* (Operating Theatre) and *Rent* (Olympia). She spent four years as costume coordinator at the Samuel Beckett Centre, Trinity College Dublin, where her work included *The Ballad of the Sad Café, Dracula, Mad Forest, The Divorcement of Figaro, 'Tis Pity She's a Whore, Artists and Admirers* and *Stages of the Nation*. Film and television work includes *Studs, Dead Bodies, Evelyn, On Home Ground, Anytime Now* and *Black Day at Blackrock*. Niamh is a graduate of Limerick College of Art and Design.

KEVIN MCFADDEN
LIGHTING DESIGN

KEVIN'S WORK AT the Abbey Theatre as lighting designer includes *The Passing, The East Pier,*

Bookworms (2012 and 2010), *Doubt, Drama at Inish, Silent, Richard II* (with Ouroboros Theatre Company), *Fool for Love, Grown Ups, What Happened Bridgie Cleary, The Guys* and *A Quiet Life*. He has also worked as design associate on *John Gabriel Borkman*, as well as many other Abbey Theatre productions, both nationally and internationally. Other work includes *The Peace Project* (Dublin Dance Festival 2012), *Cruel and Tender* (Hatch and Project Arts Centre), *Myrmidons* (Ouroboros and Samuel Beckett Theatre), *Hysteria* (b*spoke and Project Arts Centre), *Hamlet* (Gúna Nua and Project Arts Centre), *Taste* (Gúna Nua and Andrews Lane), *Bloody Poetry* (Bank of Ireland Arts Centre) and *Seven Deadly Sins* (Performance Corporation). Multimedia projects include *Food for Life* (Kevin Thornton).

DENIS CLOHESSY
SOUND DESIGN

DENIS'S WORK AT the Abbey Theatre includes *Shibari, The Government Inspector, Perve, The Rivals, The Resistible Rise of Arturo Ui, An Ideal Husband, Three Sisters, The Seafarer, Romeo and Juliet, The Crucible, Julius Caesar, Big Love, Burial at Thebes, Fool for Love* and *Woman and Scarecrow*.

Other theatre work includes *Mrs. Warren's Profession, A Woman of No Importance, My Cousin Rachel, Da, Hay Fever, Cat on a Hot Tin Roof, Death of a Salesman, All My Sons, Faith Healer, Hedda Gabler* and *Festen* (Gate Theatre), *The Importance of Being Earnest, Sodome, My Love* (Winner Best Sound Irish Times Theatre Awards 2010), *Solemn Mass for a Full Moon in Summer, Life is a Dream, Attempts on Her Life* and *Don Carlos* (Rough Magic Theatre Company), *Man of Valour* (Winner Best Design ABSOLUT Fringe Award), *Happy Days* and *Cat on a Hot Tin Roof* (The Corn Exchange), *Silent* and *The Pride of Parnell Street* (Fishamble: The New Play Company), *Hamlet* and *A Doll's House* (Second Age Theatre Company), *The Giant Blue Hand* (The Ark), *The Shawshank Redemption* (Lane Productions) and *Macbeth* and *Titus Andronicus* (Siren Productions). Film work includes music for *His and Hers, Undressing My Mother* and *Useless Dog*, for which he won Best Soundtrack at the 2005 European Short Film Biennale in Stuttgart (Venom Films). Television work includes *Gualainn le Gualainn* (Fastnet Films) and the documentary series *The Limits of Liberty* (South Wind Blows) performed by the RTÉ Concert Orchestra.

LIZ ROCHE
MOVEMENT CO-ORDINATOR

LIZ'S WORK AT the Abbey Theatre includes *Drum Belly, King Lear, Alice in Funderland, The Government Inspector, The Cherry Orchard, Burial at Thebes* and *The House of Barnarda Alba*. Liz is artistic director and choreographer of Dublin based dance company Liz Roche Company (formerly Rex Levitates). Her most recent work *Body and Forgetting* premiered at the Abbey Theatre on the Peacock stage in January 2013. Her work for the company has been performed throughout Ireland and at the South Bank Centre London, Baryshnikov Arts Centre and Judson Memorial Church New York, LEAP Festival Liverpool, Edinburgh Fringe Festival, Meet in Beijing Festival, Festival De La Nouvelle Danse Uzes and Le Centre Culturel Irlandais, Paris. She has been commissioned to make choreographies for companies including the National Ballet of China, Scottish Dance Theatre, Cois Céim Dance Theatre, Croi Glan Integrated Dance and Dance Theatre of Ireland. Other work in theatre includes *Festen* (The Gate Theatre), *The Day I Swapped My Dad for Two Goldfish* and *1742* (The Ark), *Medea* (Siren Productions) and *The Talk of the Town, Miss Julie* and *The Secret*

Garden (Landmark Productions).
Liz has worked extensively in
Opera, including productions of
The Mines of Sulphur (Wexford
Festival Opera) *Aida* (National Opera
of Korea), *Semiramide* (Rossini
Opera Festival Pesaro), *Lucia Silla*
(Opernhaus Zurich and Opera de
Nice) and *Lady Macbeth of Mtsensk,
The Silver Tassie, Queen of Spades*
and *Aida* (Opera Ireland). Liz was
Choreographer-in-Residence at The
Irish World Academy of Music and
Dance at University of Limerick from
2009 - 2012 and is also a former
board member of Theatre Forum and
former Chair of Dance Ireland.

The Abbey Theatre would like to thank the supporters of the <u>110th Anniversary</u> <u>Campaign</u> **1904–2014**

'We have established the Abbey Theatre's 110th Anniversary Fund to ensure we continue to fuel the flame our founders lit over a century ago. I am proud to be a supporter of the 110th Campaign by being a Guardian of the Abbey Theatre. With your support we can develop playwrights, support Ireland's theatre artists, engage Irish citizens and present world renowned theatre both nationally and internationally.'

Fiach Mac Conghail, Director / Stiúrthóir

CORPORATE GUARDIANS

 THE DOYLE COLLECTION

The Westbury Hotel
DUBLIN

The Doyle Collection, official hotel partner of Ireland's national theatre.

  BROWN THOMAS

Do more.

MCCANN FITZGERALD   Irish Life

 DIAGEO
IRELAND

 gravitas fundraising
AON

 Bank of Ireland accenture
High performance. Delivered. ARTHUR COX

MEDIA PARTNERS

Sunday Independent

Irish Independent

SUPPORTER OF THE NEW PLAYWRIGHTS PROGRAMME

Deloitte.

CORPORATE AMBASSADORS

Paddy Power
101 Talbot Restaurant
Bewley's
Wynn's Hotel
Abbey Travel
CRH
Conway Communications
Lafayette Cafe
Bar & Gallery
The Merrion Hotel
Baker Tilly Ryan Glennon
National Radio Cabs
The Church Café Bar
Clarion Consulting
Limited
Westin Hotels & Resorts
Manor House Hotels
of Ireland
Zero-G
Irish Poster Advertising
Bad Ass Café

CORPORATE AMBASSADORS

Spector Information
Security
ely bar & brasserie
University College Cork

CORPORATE PARTNERS

AIB
High Performance
Management

SUPPORTING CAST

Anraí Ó Braonáin
Joe Byrne
Robbi D. Holman
Susan McGrath
Oonagh Desire
Róise Goan
John Daly
Zita Byrne

GUARDIANS OF THE ABBEY

Mrs. Carmel Naughton
Sen. Fiach Mac Conghail

FELLOWS OF THE ABBEY

Frances Britton
Catherine Byrne
Sue Cielinski
Dónall Curtin
Tommy Gibbons
James Hickey
John Keane
Andrew Mackey
Eugene Magee
James McNally
Donal Moore
Pat Moylan
Elizabeth Purcell Cribbin
Marie Rogan &
Paul Moore
Mark Ryan

Abbey Theatre
Staff & Supporters

The Abbey Theatre gratefully acknowledges the financial support of the Arts Council of Ireland and the support of the Department of the Arts, Heritage and the Gaeltacht.

Archive partner of the Abbey Theatre.

If you
VALUE THEATRE
you'll love these great opportunities...

Abbey Member

BECOMING A MEMBER of the Abbey Theatre puts you at the top of the queue by giving you great discounts and free access to talks. Sign up today and enjoy Member Benefits that include:

- Half-price tickets for Abbey stage previews
- Up to €5 off tickets for Abbey Theatre productions
- Priority booking period
- Free access to the Abbey Talks

Member €25

Joint Member €40
(for two people)

...

Benefits subject to availability. For terms and conditions see www.abbeytheatre.ie.

Abbey Friend

AS A FRIEND you can enjoy all the benefits of being a Member, plus behind the scenes insight and a closer association with the Abbey Theatre. Friend Benefits also include:

- Two tickets to a production of your choice
- Invitations to Friends' nights
- Opportunity to buy tickets for Opening Night performances
- Programme listing

Friend €125

Joint Friend €230
(for two people)

...

Joint Friends get four tickets instead of two and double the invitations.

TO JOIN
Pick up a form from the Abbey Foyer, join online at www.abbeytheatre.ie or call (01) 879 7245.

SHUSH

Elaine Murphy

For Clare, Mel and Sandra…friends indeed

Characters

BREDA, *fifties*
MARIE, *sixties*
CLARE, *thirties*
IRENE, *fifties/sixties*
URSULA, *thirties/forties*

This text went to press before the end of rehearsals and so may differ slightly from the play as performed.

ACT ONE

BREDA*'s outdated kitchen is in a state of disrepair. Broken appliances have been replaced with new items but the old ones still remain, along with magazines, newspapers, a black sack of men's clothing, golf clubs and other useless bric-a-brac. A corner of the room is being used for a home office, there is a rickety desk, a couple of boxes of unopened ballpoint pens, numerous packs of highlighters, staplers and blocks of A4 paper, which are stacked one on top of the other creating a small wall. A corporate motivational picture of an eagle with the words 'Dare to Soar' hangs over the desk. There is a large bouquet of flowers with a 'Happy Birthday Mum' card proudly displayed on the coffee table, along with a half-eaten box of Ferrero Rocher, a handbag and a couple of pill bottles. Photos of* BREDA*'s son, Colm, at various stages of his life are displayed around the room, and of* BREDA *and her husband, Tommy, at a dance and on their wedding day. A stopped clock hangs on the kitchen wall.*

BREDA *is sitting in her armchair drinking vodka and looking at the pills. She is wearing dark shapeless clothes with a dressing gown. Her face is bare of make-up and her hair slightly messed. She contemplates making a call and finally dials…*

BREDA. Hi, Colm, it's Mammy… em… if you can get back to me tonight, it doesn't matter how late… not that it's an emergency or anything… it'd just be nice to talk to you on the day that's in it. Okay, love, bye.

Her phone beeps with an incoming text message.

Happy Birthday from the O2 network.

BREDA *throws the phone aside and eats another chocolate, still staring at the pills. The doorbell rings, startling her. We hear chattering outside. On realising it's her friends,* BREDA *quickly drains the remainder of her drink and clears away the pills. The doorbell rings again. Noticing the*

Ferrero Rocher, she tucks them down the side of the armchair, covering them with a cushion. She finally answers the door to MARIE, CLARE *and* IRENE, *who are all dressed for the cold winter weather.*

MARIE. Hi-di-hi.

IRENE. Ho-di-ho.

MARIE *waves out to the street.*

MARIE. She's here, I'll ring you later. (*To* BREDA.) Are we coming in or what?

Offstage, a horn beeps and a car pulls away.

BREDA. Of course, come in. What are you all doing here?

IRENE. We came to see the birthday girl.

MARIE. And if Muhammad won't come to the mountain…

BREDA. Oh, that… I'm not celebrating this year.

MARIE. You say that every year… Jaysus, it's freezing out there.

IRENE. We brought you something to help you forget.

IRENE *hands* BREDA *a large bottle of vodka.*

BREDA. That should do the trick.

IRENE. C'mere and give us a love, happy birthday.

IRENE *envelops* BREDA *in a big hug and then drags everyone else into her embrace.* MARIE *extracts herself from* IRENE's *grip.*

MARIE. Get off me, Redback.

CLARE. You don't mind us landing on you, Breda?

MARIE. I told her I'd pop over during the week.

BREDA. You could've narrowed it down for me.

IRENE. I bet you were expecting us.

BREDA. I really wasn't.

MARIE (*looking around*). Obviously.

BREDA. It's great to see you, Clare.

CLARE. You too, Breda.

BREDA. To what do I owe the pleasure?

MARIE. She's staying in mine tonight and our electricity's gone, again.

CLARE. Mam.

BREDA. I thought that was all sorted.

MARIE. It was supposed to be but it keeps coming and going, I don't know what they're at.

CLARE. It was back on when we were leaving.

MARIE. That and the telly was shite – Wha'? Irene, isn't the telly shite these days?

IRENE. It is.

MARIE. So I said you might as well come with us.

BREDA. Well, it's nice to see you anyway, Clare.

CLARE *smiles awkwardly.* MARIE *is carrying two bottles of mixers and is about to put them in the fridge…*

Give me that.

BREDA *takes the bottles from her and manoeuvres the rickety fridge door.*

MARIE. Have you not fixed that yet?

BREDA. It's on my to-do list.

MARIE. It must be a novel by now.

CLARE. The place looks… well.

IRENE. I was just thinking that.

BREDA. Thanks.

MARIE. Normally she sprays a bit of Mr Sheen in the air and calls it a day.

BREDA. You should have left her at home.

CLARE. We tried but Dad insisted we bring her.

BREDA *moves a few things around so the girls can sit down.*

IRENE. Were you having a clear-out?

BREDA. Tommy asked me to put a few of his things aside.

MARIE. That was very decent of you.

BREDA. Ah, sure. Did your daddy drop you off?

CLARE. Yeah.

MARIE. I'm not paying for a taxi with a car outside the door
    and a husband sitting at home doing nothing.

BREDA. He's very good, isn't he?

CLARE. The best.

MARIE. I have him well trained. Why don't you go on upstairs
    and wash your face while I make us all a little drinkie, what
    are we having?

CLARE. Just an orange juice for me, thanks.

MARIE. Bacardi, Irene?

IRENE *produces a large bottle of Bacardi from a shopping
    bag and hands it to* MARIE.

IRENE. A small one.

MARIE. They only had fat Coke in the shop, will that do you?

IRENE. It makes me very gassy, Marie.

MARIE. Just drink it.

IRENE. Okay so.

BREDA *is about to hand* CLARE *her juice.*

MARIE. I'll throw a vodka into that for her, Breda.

CLARE. I'm fine, thanks.

MARIE. Clare, don't be such a square.

Before CLARE *can protest,* MARIE *adds a large vodka to
    her juice.* CLARE *never has more than a few sips and is
    constantly looking for new and inventive ways to avoid
    alcohol.*

It'll do you no harm, loosen you up a bit. (*To* BREDA.) Look alive, we'll still be here when you get back.

BREDA. Oh right.

MARIE. And put something else on while you're up there.

BREDA *exits*. CLARE *looks at* MARIE.

What's with the face?

CLARE. You're as subtle as a brick.

MARIE. She has visitors and I'm sick looking at her in that jumper. She doesn't look great, does she?

IRENE. She's delicate, Marie.

MARIE. What do you think, Clare?

CLARE. I barely spoke to her.

MARIE. Well, you haven't seen her in a while... I think she looks wrecked.

CLARE. She doesn't look wrecked, Mam.

MARIE. She does...

CLARE. She looks like she could do with a break.

MARIE. She has Colm worried sick. He rang me you know –

CLARE *and* IRENE. You said.

MARIE. So what are we going to do?

CLARE. Don't start, Mam.

MARIE. We have to do something.

IRENE. We'll be here for her.

MARIE. That's not a plan. The best thing she can do for herself is get back out there – get her snap back. (*Clicks her fingers.*)

IRENE. She's not ready.

MARIE. You're never ready. I'll talk to her –

CLARE. You will not.

MARIE. She needs someone to tell it like it is –

CLARE. She's a grown woman, she'll work it out for herself.

MARIE. If I say it, it'll be like cutting through the red tape.

BREDA *enters in a black dress, her hair somewhat tamed.*

CLARE. Say nothing, I'm warning you.

CLARE *gestures for* MARIE *to keep her mouth shut.*

Ssh… promise.

MARIE. I… p–

BREDA. How's that, better?

MARIE. It's a start.

CLARE *elbows* MARIE.

Much, much better.

IRENE. Is that new?

BREDA *looks down at her dress.*

BREDA. Yeah.

IRENE. It's lovely.

BREDA. Thanks.

MARIE. What did you buy it for?

BREDA. To have.

MARIE. Do they have it in blue?

BREDA. I only saw it in black.

MARIE. Pity, blue's massive on you, I find the black a bit morbid.

CLARE. I think it's gorgeous on you, you look great.

MARIE. You do.

IRENE. That'll be the acupuncture.

MARIE *tries to warm herself at the nearby radiator but is disappointed to find it cold.*

MARIE. Any chance of you putting the heating on, it's freezing in here.

BREDA *turns the heating on by giving it a kick/thump*.

CLARE. You're getting acupuncture?

BREDA. Yeah... they put this little needle in my ear, see, and it stops me craving – the sugar.

MARIE. Clare's into all that ssshh... stuff.

BREDA. Oh really?

CLARE. Yeah, how's it going for you?

BREDA. So far so good.

IRENE. Did you go this week?

BREDA. I was there last week.

MARIE. I thought you were to go every week.

BREDA. I'd no car.

MARIE. Where is it?

BREDA. It's making this funny rattling noise, my nerves would be gone if I had to drive it.

IRENE. You should bring it to my mechanic, he's very reasonable.

BREDA. I will.

MARIE. She'll add it to the list. I would've given you a lift over.

CLARE. Who owns the big Jeep parked outside?

BREDA *notices they are still wearing their coats, they reluctantly part with them*.

BREDA. Ursula next door.

IRENE. She's a lovely girl.

MARIE. She's real affected.

BREDA. She's lovely and that husband of hers, what's he like, Irene?

IRENE. You'd ate him, Clare.

BREDA. Very attractive, gorgeous-looking couple.

MARIE. Next time I'll drop you over – I have to keep tabs on her.

BREDA. I was very good all week.

MARIE. The doctor says you have to get the weight down; she's hypertensive.

BREDA. Will you get off my back, it's my birthday.

MARIE *ignores* BREDA*'s offer of taking her coat and wraps it tightly around herself.*

IRENE (*to* BREDA). Clare was telling me all about her new house on the way over. It sounds gorgeous, is it gorgeous, Marie?

MARIE. Fabulous, yeah.

BREDA. Which reminds me, I have something for you.

BREDA *begins searching through the bric-a-brac and junk mail.*

CLARE. For me?

BREDA. Yeah, here… somewhere…

IRENE. Any shift on the old place?

CLARE. Eoin and I are landlords now.

IRENE. Sure isn't property a great investment?

CLARE. Well –

IRENE. Now come here and tell me, how many bedrooms?

CLARE. Four.

IRENE. Four, I'd love to see it.

CLARE. You'll have to come out to me.

IRENE. I will.

MARIE. You do know she'll take you up on that, don't you?

IRENE. We'll make a day of it.

MARIE. You'll have to, she's miles away.

IRENE. Any sign of you filling up them rooms?

CLARE. Not yet, no.

MARIE. Will you leave the girl alone, harassing her.

IRENE. I'm no more harassing her.

MARIE. She's the big career to think of, tell her what you are now.

CLARE. Mam... Head of Marketing.

IRENE. Head of Marketing, would you be able? Congratulations, Clare.

BREDA. Nice to see a woman breaking through, when I started in the Civil Service I had to give up my job once I got married.

MARIE. They took you back, didn't they?

BREDA. Fair play to you, you worked hard.

MARIE. She did, she worked very hard.

BREDA *hands* CLARE *the lids off three pots.*

BREDA. I knew I had them here somewhere. I've been saving the tokens for you. I'd enough for the lids and if you save up another two pages' worth, you'll have enough for the pots.

CLARE. Breda... you're as thoughtful.

BREDA. I wasn't sure whether you wanted the black or the silver, in the end I thought the silver would go with more.

CLARE. They will; thanks.

BREDA. You're welcome.

There is a knock on the door.

URSULA. Knock, knock.

BREDA. Speak of the divil – in here, Ursula.

URSULA *enters, wearing large designer sunglasses.*

URSULA. How's everyone? I didn't realise you had company.

MARIE *raises an eyebrow to* CLARE.

BREDA. Surprise... Have you met Clare, Marie's daughter?

URSULA. I haven't, lovely to meet you. I can see the resemblance.

MARIE. She's adopted.

CLARE. Mam... I am not, don't mind her, nice to meet you.

URSULA. You're a ticket, Marie.

BREDA (*admiring* URSULA*'s sunglasses*). They're lovely.

URSULA. I have an eye infection.

IRENE. Is it the conjunctivitis, Ursula?

URSULA. Something like that.

IRENE. Very uncomfortable.

URSULA. Very.

IRENE. You should get Marie to have a look at it for you, she's trained in first aid; they say she could've been a nurse.

URSULA. I've already been to the doctor, thanks, should be cleared up in no time.

IRENE. Keep an eye on that now. Do you hear me? – An eye.

URSULA *hands* BREDA *a tin and a bottle*.

URSULA. I will. We made you a little birthday cake, the kids stuck a few Smarties on it for you.

BREDA. You did not... you're too good – Max's cakes are only divine.

URSULA. The kids and I made this one.

BREDA. Oh.

URSULA. But don't worry, Max talked us through it step by step over the phone.

BREDA. I'm sure it's fantastic. You'll join us?

URSULA. I wouldn't want to intrude.

BREDA. Go on out of that. What are you having?

URSULA. I would murder a glass of rosé.

MARIE. Vodka or Bacardi.

URSULA. We could have a drop of this…

IRENE. Ohhh champers.

URSULA. Well… cava.

BREDA. You'll have to open it for me.

URSULA. Do you have a cloth?

BREDA. In there. That's a lovely tin, Ursula.

URSULA. Cute, isn't it? It's part of a set.

BREDA. Grand size and everything, very handy I'd say.

URSULA. Yeah.

BREDA. It is, it's a lovely one now, do they sell those individually I wonder?

URSULA. I don't know, it was a wedding present. (*Pause.*) You can keep it if you like.

BREDA. Are you sure?

URSULA. Of course, I have the whole range.

BREDA. Thanks, Ursula… another little pressie for me.

URSULA. Yay.

BREDA *opens a press and adds the tin to a collection of Tupperware in various shapes and sizes. As* URSULA *opens the utensil drawer the front panel comes off and she is left holding it in her hand.*

Oh my God.

BREDA. Don't mind that.

BREDA *takes the panel from* URSULA *and places it back on the drawer so it looks fixed but is actually just resting there.*

Now that's grand.

BREDA *then opens another press which is full of tea towels and hands one to* URSULA.

URSULA. Well stocked.

BREDA. You never know.

MARIE (*aside to* IRENE). Every time I pull up she just happens to be popping her head in the door.

IRENE. I invited her – it would've been rude not to and she only next door.

MARIE. This party was supposed to be just for us.

IRENE. Breda doesn't even know she's at a party.

URSULA *pops the cork.* MARIE *gets a fright.*

MARIE. 'Sake.

BREDA *and* URSULA *fill a glass for everyone.* CLARE *discreetly empties her vodka down the sink,* URSULA *replaces it almost immediately with a glass of cava.*

URSULA. What are we like and on a school night?

MARIE. Mad.

URSULA. I know. *Sláinte.*

ALL. *Sláinte.*

IRENE. Don't you just love bubbles.

MARIE. More than life itself.

IRENE. How are all your lot, Ursula?

URSULA. Fabulous, getting big and bold.

CLARE. How old are they?

URSULA. Jake's six –

MARIE. You're like Madonna sitting there, will you let the air at it.

MARIE *attempts to grab* URSULA*'s glasses but* URSULA *catches her in time and reluctantly pushes the sunglasses back into her hair.*

IRENE. Oh, that is nasty, Ursula.

IRENE *moves in for closer inspection.*

URSULA. It looks a lot worse than it is – as I was saying,
    Irene… Aaron is three and Ciara will be one on Sunday.

IRENE. It's Bobby's anniversary on Sunday too.

BREDA. It's never.

URSULA. Bobby?

BREDA. Irene's second husband.

URSULA. Oh, I'm so sorry.

IRENE. Fifteen years ago now.

BREDA. It doesn't feel that long, does it feel that long to you,
    Irene?

IRENE. It does and it doesn't.

MARIE. Lovely man, he'd nearly fall off his bike to say hello
    to you.

BREDA. Always sang 'Sweet Caroline' with the few jars on him.

IRENE. With not a note in his head. And Ciara a year already, it
    seems like only yesterday you were out to here on her.

URSULA. Thirteen pounds, four ounces.

CLARE. Good God.

BREDA. I know and the little figure on her.

URSULA. At one stage I thought she was going to get up and
    walk out of my womb, sure she's nearly as tall as Aaron
    already.

BREDA. You'd want to see her though, Clare; she's a gorgeous
    little… big thing.

CLARE. I'd say you've your hands full.

URSULA. Like you wouldn't believe.

IRENE. Have you any photos to show Clare?

URSULA. I'm sure I do.

IRENE. Wait until you see her, Clare.

URSULA. Here she is just after she was born…

URSULA *drains her glass while* CLARE *looks at photos on her phone.*

CLARE. Whoa… she is so cute.

IRENE. You poor thing, Ursula.

URSULA *gestures for a caesarean.*

URSULA. Sunroof.

MARIE. Thank God for small mercies.

URSULA. The lads with their sister…

BREDA. Ah, she's crying.

URSULA. Aaron's probably pinching her. Max and Ciara…

BREDA. A daddy's girl, huh?

MARIE. I know another one of them. Give us a look, she is beautiful, Ursula.

IRENE. She is.

BREDA. Tell Clare what you do on a Thursday morning.

URSULA. What do I do?

BREDA. The yoga thing…

URSULA. Oh, yeah… baby yoga.

BREDA. Baby yoga. Isn't it great what they have the kids doing nowadays and tell her what else you do.

URSULA. I… eh… what else do I do?

BREDA. The thing… the sign-language thing.

URSULA. Baby sign?

BREDA. Baby sign, show her a bit.

URSULA. No.

BREDA. Ah, go on, it's brilliant.

URSULA. Clare's no interest in –

CLARE. I'd love to see it.

URSULA *demonstrates sign language for the following:*

URSULA. Okay… 'Milk', 'cat', 'dog'.

CLARE. That's great.

IRENE. When did you find out, Ursula?

URSULA. About what?

IRENE. That Ciara's deaf.

URSULA. She's not deaf.

IRENE. No?

URSULA. It's so she can communicate before she talks.

IRENE. Oh right.

BREDA. Isn't it amazing?

IRENE. Amazing.

BREDA. And Aaron's in Montessori and Jake's in everything at the school; isn't he, Ursula?

URSULA. Busy household alright. Which one is mine?

CLARE *pushes her full glass towards* URSULA, *pretending* URSULA*'s empty glass is her own.* MARIE, *noticing* CLARE*'s glass is now empty, refills it almost immediately.*

MARIE. Top-up?

CLARE. I've enough.

MARIE. You can nurse that one too.

BREDA. I don't know how you do it. I'm knackered just looking at you.

URSULA. I've had to rein it in a bit since I went back to work.

MARIE. I didn't know you were back in work.

URSULA. I missed it, you know.

BREDA. Superwoman, what?

URSULA. Anything to escape the madness.

MARIE. I started a new job there myself, Ursula.

URSULA. Fabulous, where?

MARIE. In the supermarket up beside Irene.

URSULA. How's it all going?

MARIE. Great.

CLARE. Tell her about Diane.

MARIE. I call her Daisy, because she's like a cow... (*Mimes chewing gum.*) I've finished my training with her.

IRENE. Already? That was very fast.

URSULA. A quick learner is always very valuable in the workplace, Marie.

CLARE. Diane told Mam to stop talking.

MARIE. Easier said than done... I was meeting people up there I hadn't seen in years... I couldn't not talk to them and they filling me in on all the gossip. You'll never guess who I met, only Catherine Brady.

IRENE. How is she?

MARIE. She looks great... considering. She was asking after you, Breda.

BREDA. Was she now?

MARIE. Heard you were going through a tough time.

BREDA. Delighted, I bet.

MARIE. Don't be like that, she's back living up around our way, St Dympna's I think she said.

BREDA. Since when?

MARIE. This last year. She was saying some car accident caused the power cuts.

BREDA. Really? And what else did she say?

MARIE. That was as far as she got cos didn't Daisy interrupt us. She was annoying me something fierce and the gnawing out of her, by lunchtime I said: 'See you, Daisy, pop that gum in my ear one more time and I'll choke you.' She was supposed to shadow me for a few days but signed off at the end of the first. Suited me, but I haven't figured out how to balance my till yet.

URSULA. Permanent contract?

MARIE. Two-week trial – I forgot you worked in recruitment; I'll drop into you if it doesn't work out.

URSULA. Let's hope there'll be no need for that.

IRENE. How are things going in your place, Breda?

BREDA. The atmosphere is still terrible.

MARIE. There's nothing worse.

BREDA. I've decided to take early retirement.

MARIE. You're joking.

BREDA. No, they're downsizing the department and we all have to reapply for our positions.

CLARE. Can they do that, Breda?

BREDA. Apparently, they can do what they like.

MARIE. Cheek of them, after how many years?

BREDA. Twenty-six.

MARIE. You've no idea of the stress she's been under.

BREDA. It's a relief, to be honest, people I would've considered friends are turning on each other, afraid of their lives they'll be next for the bullet.

MARIE. I bet you Mary Ellen is staying put.

BREDA. Don't you know.

CLARE. Who's this?

MARIE. Her boss, she's some rip, isn't she, Breda?

BREDA. Fecking gilly – working every hour God sends for half of what they were paying yer man before her.

URSULA. What about a transfer?

BREDA. No, I couldn't be bothered at this stage of my life, the package is good and if I leave it any longer there may not be any money to take.

IRENE. Are you getting a party?

BREDA. End of the month.

IRENE *is delighted by this.*

IRENE. Can we come?

BREDA. Well, it's more of a lunch, staff only I'm afraid – the money isn't there for the big parties any more.

MARIE. They don't want to drag the arse out of it, you mean.

BREDA. Now you have it.

MARIE. That's very disappointing… are you very disappointed?

BREDA. I am a bit but you know what, bigger fool me, at the end of the day you're only ever a number.

MARIE. Isn't that the truth.

URSULA. If you like I could help you with your CV, spruce it up a bit before you start sending it out again.

IRENE. That'd be wonderful, Ursula, wouldn't that be wonderful, Breda?

BREDA. Brillo.

IRENE. I could do with a few tips myself.

MARIE. What's wrong with the dry-cleaners?

IRENE. Nothing, but it's good to know these things, I'll get you a bit of paper.

BREDA. We don't need to get into all that now…

IRENE *takes a page from the stack of paper and searches for a pen.*

IRENE. Have you a pen, Breda?

BREDA. In front of you.

IRENE. Where?

BREDA *joins her and picks up one of the unopened box of pens.*

Right under my nose, jeez… you've loads.

IRENE *looks at the picture of the eagle while* BREDA *opens the box of pens and hands her one.*

'Dare to Soar'…

BREDA. I got that out of the job.

MARIE. Were they throwing them out, Breda?

BREDA.… Yeah.

IRENE. I thought parrots couldn't fly.

BREDA. That's an eagle.

IRENE. Is that what that is?

MARIE. Are you ever going to wear your glasses?

IRENE. No, I hate them.

MARIE. You're so vain.

BREDA. And parrots can fly.

IRENE. Can they?

BREDA. Of course they can, they're birds. What made you think they couldn't?

IRENE. I don't know, I heard it somewhere…

BREDA. They can't if you clip their wings.

IRENE. Why would you clip their wings?

BREDA. Stop them flying.

IRENE. That's terrible.

BREDA. I'm sure there's a picture of a dolphin in the boardroom, I'll get you that if you like.

IRENE. That'd be lovely, thanks, Breda. Black or blue, Ursula?

URSULA. Blue…

URSULA *begins sketching sections on a page.*

MARIE. Give us a look now, see if I've been doing mine right.

CLARE. Yeah, you should really know how to do this properly.

URSULA. Okay, so you'll have all your personal information here and then work experience… here… so…?

BREDA. I've only ever had the one job.

URSULA. How did you get away with that?

BREDA. I did the exam after secretarial school, went straight in, took a few years off when Colm was born and went back.

URSULA. And have you held the same position all this time?

BREDA. Ah no, I moved around.

MARIE. Tell her about all your courses, she's degrees coming out of her ears.

BREDA. Hardly… well, I've a few.

CLARE. In what?

BREDA. BA in Business Studies, Diploma in Leadership and Management – the job paid for that – and then I did a few of those introductory courses like Humanities, History…

MARIE. Tell her about the thing you were doing up in Glasnevin Cemetery.

BREDA. Which…? Oh, that was just a history thing.

MARIE. It was about the fellas from the 1916 Rising. Did you ever finish it?

BREDA. Not yet no.

MARIE. It sounded very interesting, didn't it, Irene?

IRENE. It did, yeah.

MARIE. I'm telling you, brains to burn this one.

BREDA. And then there was the in-house training I did, anything to get out of the office for the day. I have all the certificates somewhere. (*Taking the pen and paper from* URSULA.)

I'll have a root during the week, there's no hurry, I'm going to take a few weeks off first... reassess.

CLARE. This could turn out to be a great opportunity for you, Breda.

MARIE. Are you for real?

CLARE. Mam, where one door closes a window opens.

IRENE. I agree with Clare –

MARIE. You would.

CLARE. This could be the start of bigger and better things for you.

MARIE. Like what?

CLARE. She could start her own business.

BREDA. I'm not starting any business, I've a pain in my arse working.

CLARE. You could go travelling.

IRENE. This calls for a celebration.

IRENE *jumps up to organise the presents.*

BREDA. Where?

CLARE. Wherever you want.

BREDA. I don't think I'd be into that.

URSULA *prepares herself a vodka and mixer while organising the cake.*

URSULA. Shall we cut the cake?

IRENE. Presents first.

BREDA. You got me presents?

MARIE. Don't look so surprised.

BREDA. There was no need for that.

IRENE. Aren't you worth it?

CLARE *goes first.*

CLARE. There you go, Breda.

BREDA *carefully opens the wrapping paper and bow and puts them to one side to save. It's a big box of Ferrero Rocher.*

IRENE. Your favourite.

CLARE. Sorry, Breda, I didn't know about your ear thing.

BREDA. I haven't had these in ages, thanks, Clare.

MARIE *grabs them off her.*

MARIE. You needn't think you're getting stuck into them, birthday or no birthday.

CLARE. Mam…

IRENE. She can have one.

MARIE *reluctantly hands the chocolates back to* BREDA.

BREDA. We'll share them… later.

BREDA *puts the chocolates away.* IRENE *hands* BREDA *her gift in a fancy bag,* BREDA *admiring the bag, puts it to one side with the wrapping paper. It's a helmet disguised as a hood.*

IRENE. What do you think?

BREDA. It's lovely. What is it?

IRENE. A Snuddie.

BREDA. A what?

IRENE *models the hood.*

IRENE. A Snuddie – a snuggly hoodie. You can attach it to anything, see?

IRENE *bangs her head off the table.*

It protects your head when you're out walking.

BREDA. Very… handy.

MARIE. She doesn't go walking.

IRENE. She does.

MARIE. Since when?

BREDA. Since the needle fella recommended it.

MARIE. Good for you.

IRENE. Show her your head.

BREDA. I slipped on ice in the driveway, stupid.

MARIE. C'mere to me.

BREDA. Marie, it's grand.

MARIE. I'm fully trained, relax.

> MARIE *pins* BREDA *to the chair and feels her scalp, ignoring her protests.*

> Where? There?

BREDA. Go easy.

MARIE. That's some lump.

IRENE. Didn't she get a right whack?

MARIE. I told you to get that Cobble Lock done, it's brilliant, isn't it brilliant, Irene?

IRENE. Brilliant, yeah.

URSULA. One of the first things we did when we moved in.

IRENE. You could even get a little rockery with a flower bed.

BREDA. I don't want the feckin Cobble Lock done, it was an accident.

URSULA. Where do you keep the plates, Breda?

BREDA. Over there.

> URSULA *reaches to open the nearest cupboard, as she does so, the kick-board along the fitted kitchen falls down with a loud snap, like a domino effect.*

URSULA. Oh my God, what is with me tonight?

BREDA. Just kick them out of the way, Ursula.

CLARE *leaves her drink on the countertop to help* URSULA *with the plates. When finished,* URSULA, *thinking the glass is hers, picks it up and returns to her seat.* CLARE *follows, pleased with herself for offloading more alcohol.*

MARIE. Last but not least.

BREDA *is delicately unwrapping her present when* MARIE *leans forward and rips it off, leaving the paper unsalvageable. It's a pair of ballroom-dancing shoes.* BREDA *is put out.*

There's a voucher in there for your first lesson. Do you not like them?

BREDA. They're lovely.

MARIE. If you don't like them I can take them back. I'll take them back.

MARIE *puts them back in the box.* BREDA *takes them back out of the box.*

BREDA. I like them.

MARIE. You used to be a brilliant dancer.

MARIE *puts the shoes on her hands and dances them across the table.* IRENE *watches the shoes, wincing every time they touch the table.*

BREDA. Brilliant's pushing it.

BREDA *tops up her glass.*

(*To* CLARE.) Where's your glass?

CLARE. I'm fine for the minute thanks, Breda.

MARIE. Get her another one.

BREDA *fetches* CLARE *a clean glass and mixes her a drink.*

I was there when you took home the cup.

URSULA. You got a cup?

MARIE. Butlins 1993.

BREDA. I was up against two other mammies from Liverpool and one from Aberdeen, it was hardly *Strictly*.

CLARE. Was that the year I won the hula-hoop competition?

MARIE. It was, it was the year we cleaned up. Great oul holiday, wasn't it, Breda?

BREDA. It pissed rain for most of it.

CLARE. Didn't Colm give someone a dig for some reason?

MARIE. Breda's dance partner, the redcoat fella, no doubt he deserved it.

BREDA. That's right, do you remember the pair of you came back from the teenage disco, locked?

MARIE. Even then you couldn't handle your drink, Clare.

CLARE. And yet you still can't get it down my neck quick enough.

MARIE. You didn't need it back then, you were good craic. Those were the days, Breda, wha'?

BREDA. I can barely remember it, it feels like a lifetime ago.

MARIE. Your son does, still walking around with those mental images of his mother dirty dancing.

BREDA. He wasn't the only who had too much cider that night.

URSULA. Have we only the one candle?

MARIE. No point setting off the smoke alarm.

BREDA. She knows from experience.

IRENE *grabs the shoes off* MARIE *and puts them back in the box.*

IRENE. It's bad luck to have shoes on the table.

MARIE. You're bad luck, Redback.

BREDA. Stop calling her that.

MARIE. She knows I'm only joking, don't you know I'm only joking?

IRENE. I do.

URSULA. Where did you get Redback from anyway?

MARIE. When Irene got sunburned in Croatia – what was your back like?

IRENE. Awful.

MARIE. Awful, like the crackling on a Sunday joint. Bernard started calling her Redback and it just stuck, didn't it?

IRENE. It did.

> URSULA *unveils the cake*.

URSULA. Ta-dah.

CLARE. Happy Birthday…

> *The rest of the girls join in with 'to you'…*

BREDA. Move it on.

> IRENE *finishes the song at high speed*.

IRENE.…Happy birthday to you and many more. Blow.

BREDA. You do it for me.

> *As* IRENE *is more excited about the cake,* BREDA *signals for* IRENE *to blow out the candle instead*.

> Did you make me a wish?

IRENE. Yep, I –

MARIE. In your head.

BREDA. Was it a good one?

IRENE. The best.

> URSULA *begins dishing cake out to everyone*.

> What kind is it, Ursula?

URSULA. Chocolate.

IRENE. Very fattening.

URSULA. Organic flour, free-range eggs, eighty per cent fairtrade cocoa it's practically good for you, Irene.

IRENE. Well then…

MARIE. Trust you to find chocolate that's good for you.

BREDA. I'd better not. Are you not having any yourself, Ursula?

URSULA. I haven't much more to lose now.

BREDA. You didn't have much to start.

URSULA. I'll stick to my liquid diet, thanks.

> MARIE *and* IRENE *take large forkfuls of cake.*

IRENE. What time are you in tomorrow, Ursula?

URSULA. I'm ringing in sick.

MARIE. You'd want to be careful now, you're only back a wet day.

URSULA. You let me worry about that, Marie.

> MARIE *and* IRENE *begin to realise the cake tastes awful.*

CLARE. Are you working tomorrow?

MARIE. Not till lunchtime.

IRENE. Is it a new recipe you're using, Ursula?

URSULA. Same one. Do you mind if I help myself to another drink, Breda?

BREDA. Work away.

URSULA. And another little drop for Clare.

CLARE. Honestly, I'm grand.

> URSULA, *ignoring* CLARE, *refills her glass and then her own.*

MARIE. Try some of that.

CLARE. You know I don't like cake.

BREDA. How could you not like cake?

MARIE. I told you she's gone weird.

CLARE. I'm hardly weird, Mam.

MARIE. Torments herself over a few drinks.

IRENE. What would you normally have now, Clare?

CLARE. I like teas: green, raspberry, ginger… they're great for your digestive system.

MARIE draws an imaginary square.

Gimme that.

CLARE is about to grab MARIE's fork…

MARIE. Are you sure? It's not kosher or whatever the new faddy diet is now.

CLARE. Kosher isn't a faddy diet, Mam.

MARIE hands her the fork.

MARIE. I know, I know, 'it's a way of life', isn't that what they're always saying to you in WeightWatchers, Breda?

BREDA is too busy debating whether she should take a piece to notice CLARE spitting the cake into a napkin.

BREDA. I might have just a little nibble.

IRENE. Here, have the last bit of mine.

MARIE. Don't.

IRENE. It's only a little bit.

BREDA. Yeah, it's only a little bit, Marie.

MARIE. Your ear thing, she could have a reaction to the sugar.

IRENE. There's no sugar in that.

CLARE. It'll be easier if you just get it out of your sight.

BREDA. Do you think?

CLARE. Yeah.

BREDA. Right so. I'm putting it away, Ursula, if I start I won't stop.

URSULA. That good, huh?

ALL. Hmmm…

While clearing away the cake, BREDA sneaks a lump into her mouth.

CLARE. Have you ever heard of the tapping technique, Breda?

BREDA's mouth is full of cake, a couple of seconds in, she realises it tastes awful.

BREDA. Hmm...?

CLARE. I did a course on it. It's brilliant for cravings and stressful situations. I'll show it to you, follow me, right?

BREDA. Hmm...

CLARE. Tap under the eye... collarbone... back of your hand... close your eyes... open them... look left... look right... count: one, two, three, four, five.

CLARE takes a deep cleansing breath.

How do you feel?

BREDA gives her the thumbs up.

MARIE. You can swallow that lump of cake in your gob now, Breda.

BREDA reluctantly swallows.

IRENE. Did your job show you that, in case you burn out?

CLARE. I've been doing a course at night.

IRENE. To be a tapper?

CLARE. Holistic healer.

BREDA. Your mammy never said.

CLARE. I'll be needing a few guinea pigs soon, if you're interested.

BREDA. Sounds great.

IRENE. You should talk to the girl in Nature's Way, she gave me these great tablets for my prostate.

CLARE. Prostate?

IRENE. The doctor syringed it and everything but it made no difference.

CLARE. Sounds horrendous.

IRENE. It was.

BREDA *grabs the unopened iPod that has been sitting in a box on top of the broken stereo.*

BREDA. Will you get that going for me, Clare?

IRENE. What is it?

BREDA. Music thing, Colm sent it from New York along with the flowers.

URSULA. They're beautiful.

IRENE. They are.

BREDA. Sure he has me spoiled rotten. I saw the delivery man dropping off a big bouquet to your door yesterday. Was it your anniversary or something?

URSULA. No.

BREDA. What were they for?

URSULA. Max just sent them.

BREDA. And they say romance is dead, he's a smooth operator that one.

URSULA. He sure is.

CLARE. He has all the music on it for you and everything, Breda.

BREDA. Brillo.

CLARE *plays some music in the background.*

CLARE. How is Colm, these days?

BREDA. Great, he's working for this health-care company now, landed on his feet he did.

MARIE. Colm's the type, Ursula, if he fell into the River Liffey he'd come up with a salmon in his mouth.

CLARE. He was always very clever in school. Is he still with the same girl?

BREDA. Alice, yeah, lovely girl, I think she could be the one.

MARIE. If there's one, there'll be another.

BREDA. You've been married to the same man for thirty-four years.

MARIE *makes a shush/nod in* CLARE'*s direction.*

MARIE. Thirty-five.

BREDA. He'll never come home now.

IRENE. Sure isn't this what it's all about, seeing him happy.

BREDA. I'd rather he was here.

MARIE. You'll have to take a little trip over, won't you?

CLARE. The perfect place to start your travels.

BREDA. I'm not getting on a plane by myself.

URSULA. Maybe Tommy will go with you, a little holiday might be exactly what you need to get back on track.

BREDA. I think we're beyond that, Ursula.

URSULA. He'll come to his senses, they always do.

BREDA. He moved into a new house.

URSULA. When?

BREDA. Two weeks ago.

URSULA. I knew things weren't great but I didn't realise they were this bad.

MARIE. If Bernard was carrying on with that yoke I'd stab him in his sleep.

URSULA. He left for someone else?

BREDA. They always leave for someone else.

MARIE. 'Teresa the Tramp.'

IRENE. She's no oil painting.

BREDA. She looks like the back of a bus.

MARIE. She's definitely the size of one, she has a pair of spades [hands] like Jack Charlton.

BREDA. There's some comfort getting traded in for a younger model, but for that yoke…

IRENE. She wasn't the start of your troubles.

BREDA. She cemented them.

URSULA. How long has this been going on?

BREDA. Who knows? But I knew someone would raise their ugly head, there was no way he was leaving this place for a bedsit in Rathmines.

URSULA. Oh God.

BREDA. You know we hadn't been together for a while… this suited us financially.

IRENE. It would have suited you more if you won the Lotto.

MARIE. Or if the fucker died.

BREDA. God forbid the bastard would do something useful. I got a letter from his solicitor, he wants to sell the house.

IRENE. He never…

MARIE. You can't let him, Breda.

BREDA. He'd like a quick sale.

CLARE. I've had two viewings in fifteen months, he hasn't a hope.

MARIE. This house would be gone in a flash, it's apartments like yours nobody wants… though you might be lucky, Breda, people expect turn-key condition now…

URSULA. Where did he move to, Breda?

BREDA. Her mother's old house, not spitting distance from here.

URSULA. You're kidding.

BREDA. I wish I was, Ursula, I wish I was.

MARIE. Whereabouts?

BREDA. The avenue, the one on the corner.

MARIE. That place is in bits.

BREDA. Not any more it's not.

MARIE. Have you seen it?

BREDA. Irene saw it, said it's all done up.

IRENE. They have it lovely.

URSULA. Does this mean you'll to have to move out?

BREDA. I've no intention, Ursula. If I know Tommy, the novelty will wear off as soon as he sees her big knickers on the rad, he'll be banging down that door to get back in.

CLARE. And you'd be okay with that?

BREDA. Unfortunately it's his house too, Clare.

CLARE. I don't know whether I could handle that.

BREDA. You're young, you'd be surprised what you get used to.

URSULA. You know if you ever need anything, I'm only next door.

BREDA. I do. Don't you be worrying about me, Ursula, I'm well used to his shenanigans, let's just say this isn't the first time.

URSULA. When was the first time?

BREDA. Now there's a question... the first time I became suspicious was when he started having chats in the cloakroom under the stairs. There were no 'Bat Phones' in those days, every time the house phone rang he leapt on it. One day I hit redial and heard her voice. It turned out he was seeing this one from around the back of Fairfield. I was sick. It's one thing suspecting but it's another thing knowing, once you know, you have to do something about it.

MARIE. And that she did...

CLARE. What did you do?

MARIE. Tell her...

BREDA. I will not.

CLARE *and* URSULA. Ah, come on. / Go on.

MARIE. I'll tell them. She was on the way home from the pub one night when she happened to be passing your woman's house –

CLARE. Just happened to be passing...?

MARIE. Wait until you hear… and she noticed the bedroom light was still on. It seemed as good a time as any to confront the pair of them –

IRENE. Marie…

MARIE. – so she knocked in, nearly took the door off the hinges. When she answered, Breda pushed right by her and went straight up the stairs to catch him in the act but he wasn't around. So she locked herself in the bathroom and said she wasn't leaving until the lying scumbag showed his face.

URSULA. Did he show up?

MARIE. Nope, police did though. Turns out, she'd knocked into the wrong house.

BREDA. I called into 21 instead of 27. Gobshite like me, when I think of it…

URSULA. Why did you take him back?

BREDA. For my family, Ursula, little did I know in his mind he thought I'd granted him a licence.

IRENE. You did what you thought was best at the time.

MARIE. I swear if it was Bernard I'd slit him from here to here.

BREDA. After that it was easier to ignore, no use upsetting myself.

URSULA. Do you regret that?

BREDA. He was a good father, a shite husband but a good father and I'm glad Colm had that. I just happened to waste the best years of my life on him, eejit that I am.

MARIE. I'm not listening to that talk, for all you know the best years of your life are ahead of you.

URSULA. You'll be okay, won't you, Breda?

BREDA. Don't worry about me, Ursula. What goes around comes around –

MARIE. Ain't that the truth. She'll be grand, hasn't she all of us to keep her going?

Roberta Flack's 'Killing Me Softly' plays in the background.

IRENE. Here's your song, Marie.

MARIE. Turn it up.

IRENE. Have you ever heard Marie sing this, Ursula?

CLARE. Murder it you mean.

IRENE. She sings it lovely. Go on, Marie...

MARIE. I'm not drunk enough yet.

   MARIE *pretends to be shy but is dying to sing along.*

CLARE. Don't encourage her.

IRENE. Ah go on, for Breda, for her birthday...

   MARIE *launches into a well-rehearsed verse. At the
   appropriate time,* CLARE *intercuts with the Fugees' cover
   version, rapping: 'One time.'* MARIE, *unimpressed, ignores*
   CLARE *and carries on singing.* URSULA, *noticing how
   much* CLARE's *contribution winds* MARIE *up, joins in and
   raps: 'Two times.'* MARIE's *singing gets louder to drown out
   the girls.*

CLARE *and* URSULA. With his songgggggg...

MARIE. You're making a laugh out of me.

CLARE. We're not.

MARIE. Feck off, the lot of yis.

IRENE. I still don't know what she's going on about in that song.

MARIE. It's about her getting smothered with a pillow.

IRENE. Really?

MARIE. True as God.

BREDA. Leave Irene alone, you.

MARIE. Will you try on your shoes, please?

BREDA. What, now?

MARIE. I want to see if they fit you.

BREDA. I'm knackered, Marie.

MARIE. You're always knackered.

BREDA. I've been out working all day.

MARIE. You won't be able to use that excuse much longer, put them on you.

URSULA. Anyone else for a refill?

IRENE. A small one.

BREDA *puts on the shoes*.

MARIE. How do they feel?

BREDA. They're too high.

MARIE *puts her hand out*.

I won't be able to dance in them.

MARIE. Humour me.

BREDA *reluctantly joins her, both take the lady's stance*.

BREDA. You be the man.

MARIE. You know I can't tell the difference between my left and my right.

MARIE *leads*.

BREDA. Straighten your arms.

MARIE. She's giving out to me already.

BREDA. Start on your left.

MARIE *waits for the beat and lifts her right leg to begin*.

Your other left…

They waltz around, BREDA *is quite good,* MARIE *shuffles along*.

URSULA. She's pretty good.

MARIE. Award winning, I'll have you know.

The music speeds up as their dance routine picks up pace.
BREDA *and* MARIE *get overenthusiastic with their routine*.

CLARE. Go easy, you pair.

MARIE. Shurrup, you.

BREDA. Dip me.

MARIE. I will in my arse.

BREDA. It's my birthday, dip me.

MARIE dips her but BREDA *loses her balance.*

Are you trying to kill me?

BREDA *clutches on to the radiator to break her fall.*

MARIE. Hold on.

BREDA. I am.

The old radiator breaks away from the wall, a spray of water springs from the pipe, drowning them both. BREDA *falls.*

MARIE. You wally.

BREDA. You dropped me.

URSULA. I'll get some tea towels.

URSULA *throws them some tea towels from the pile in the press.*

BREDA. I told you they'd come in handy.

MARIE. Come on, get up.

BREDA. I'm trying.

They help BREDA *up, she tries to put weight on her foot but loses her balance.*

MARIE. Oh Jaysus, show me.

They prop her up in a chair and fuss around her. URSULA *switches off the loud music.*

BREDA. Don't come near me, you, you've done enough damage.

MARIE. I only want to look at it.

BREDA. You're too rough.

MARIE. I'm fully trained I'll have you know.

CLARE. It could be broken, Breda.

BREDA. You can look at it, Clare.

MARIE. I'll supervise so.

CLARE *examines her foot while* MARIE *looks on.*

CLARE. Can you move it from side to side?

BREDA *tries but it doesn't move.*

Are you moving it?

BREDA. Is it not?

CLARE. Can you feel this?

BREDA. I can't really feel anything, it's numb.

URSULA *tops up her own glass and passes* BREDA *another drink.*

URSULA. Here, make sure it stays that way.

MARIE. It's only a sprain.

CLARE. Is that your expert opinion?

MARIE. Should we put one of your healing crystals on it?

CLARE. She needs to go to A&E.

MARIE. Are you for real?

BREDA. I'd be seen quicker at a free clinic in Bangladesh.

IRENE. We'll tell them you work for the Government.

MARIE. All the more reason to leave her sitting there.

CLARE. You'll be crippled in the morning.

MARIE. She'll be grand; I'll bring you down to Dr Lally tomorrow, you can go back on the sick.

IRENE. She can't go on the sick, she's retiring soon.

MARIE. Might as well, I wouldn't do anything for the feckers for the last few weeks.

CLARE. Give me your scarf.

MARIE. I'm freezing.

MARIE *reluctantly hands over her scarf and watches closely as* CLARE *ties the scarf around* BREDA*'s ankle.*

CLARE. You're putting me off.

MARIE *moves away to monitor proceedings from a distance.*

BREDA. Between my hypertension and everything else, if I was a horse I'd be a Pritt Stick by now.

MARIE. By the time you get to our age you're a crock.

BREDA. I'm not your age.

MARIE. You might as well be.

IRENE *extends her arms to give* BREDA *a 'love'.* BREDA *accepts.*

IRENE. Don't mind her, Breda.

MARIE. What did I do?

CLARE. Where should we start?

Pause.

BREDA. What's his house like?

IRENE. Tommy's?… I only passed by… he was doing a bit of work in the garden at the time.

BREDA. You didn't stop and talk to him?

IRENE. God no, I gave him the nod, like this… 'Tommy'…

IRENE *passes a curt nod to an imaginary Tommy.*

MARIE. Good for you, Irene.

BREDA. What kind of work?

IRENE. Clearing it out, planting things…

BREDA. Diarmuid Gavin he is now, the bastard wouldn't even cut the grass in his own house.

MARIE. And all the times my kids came over to clear out that garden with Colm…

BREDA. I know.

MARIE. I feel duped.

BREDA. You and me both, Marie.

CLARE. He did pay us.

BREDA. I suppose she was there too…

IRENE. She had her back to me, she was at the flower beds.

BREDA. Fecking flowers beds an' all now…

MARIE. With hands like hers I doubt she needed a trowel, Breda.

IRENE. And they've a Cobble Lock driveway, with a fountain and a marble statue of an interwining couple –

BREDA. You're joking.

MARIE. State of them.

URSULA. It sounds awful, Breda.

IRENE. Actually, it's lovely, very artistic…

BREDA. Isn't it well for him and him trying to sell this place from under me.

MARIE. Bastard.

BREDA. Bastard.

MARIE. The sooner you're rid of him the better.

BREDA. Who are you telling?

MARIE. If I were you, I'd pack up all his stuff and drop it off, right in his new fountain.

BREDA. I should.

MARIE. I would. I wouldn't let him away with anything any more.

BREDA. You're right.

　　BREDA *begins throwing all Tommy's belongings into a box.*

　　What have I been waiting for?

CLARE. What are you doing?

BREDA. What I should have done years ago, I'm getting rid of him once and for all.

MARIE. That's the girl, take control.

BREDA. I will.

MARIE. He's been dictating to you for far too long.

BREDA. He has.

> BREDA *picks up a professional camera with an extra-long zoom lens and throws it in the box. Then thinks differently and pulls it back out, leaving it aside.*

CLARE. Now's not the time –

MARIE. Leave her, Clare, it's therapeutic. Wait, what are you doing?

BREDA. I'm keeping it.

IRENE. For what?

BREDA. It's mine, I bought it for him.

IRENE. Do you know how to use it?

MARIE. She can't even work the camera on her phone.

> *In another box* BREDA *finds the book:* Photography for Dummies.

BREDA. Ha, I'll learn.

> BREDA *keeps the book aside with her other items.*

MARIE. No, out, out, feck it out.

IRENE. Would you not let him have it, Breda?

> BREDA *and* MARIE *look at* IRENE *like she's insane.* BREDA *then hauls the set of golf clubs onto her back and, clutching a black bag of clothes, heads for the door.*

CLARE. Where are you going?

BREDA. To give him his stuff, I'm not waiting around for him to grace me with his presence.

MARIE. I'll go with you, I'm dying to see this garden.

URSULA. Me too, it sounds monstrous.

CLARE (*to* BREDA). You can't even walk.

> URSULA *jumps up and pulls out her keys.*

URSULA. I'll drive.

IRENE. You will not.

URSULA. You're right, I'm hammered.

MARIE *grabs the keys from* URSULA. URSULA *crumples and nods off to sleep.*

MARIE. I will.

CLARE. Mam.

CLARE *extends her hand.* MARIE *draws an imaginary square behind her back,* CLARE *catches her.*

I saw that.

MARIE *eventually hands the keys over.* CLARE *sets them aside.* BREDA *puts on her coat.*

Why are you doing this to yourself?

BREDA. I have to see it, Clare. I hear all this talk but I won't believe it until I see it with my own two eyes. I've been ignoring all of this for far too long.

MARIE. She needs closure, don't you, Breda?

BREDA. Yeah, closure.

MARIE *slyly retrieves the keys.*

MARIE. So she can move on, isn't that right, Breda?

BREDA. Yeah, move on.

MARIE. She has to see it, just this once –

BREDA. I need to see it… just this once.

CLARE. This is a terrible idea and I'll have no part of it.

MARIE. Who asked you? Come on, we'll get a taxi out on the road.

BREDA *begins walking again with the clubs on her back.*

BREDA. I can't carry…

MARIE. We'll drop those off another day, tonight we'll just do a drive-by, like we're in the hood.

MARIE drags a limping BREDA out the door. CLARE watches them leave in disbelief.

CLARE. They'll be back as soon as the cold air hits them…

IRENE looks unconvinced.

There's no way my mother would pay for a taxi, Irene.

IRENE. You're right.

CLARE, realising, jumps up to look for the keys. She flings open the front door and we hear the start up of the car engine.

CLARE. Shit! I'm going to kill her. Wait… wait… I'll drive! I'll drive!

She throws IRENE her coat.

IRENE. Are you okay to drive, Clare?

CLARE. I've been pacing myself.

URSULA. Hic.

CLARE. Come on.

They race out the door after BREDA and MARIE, leaving a sleeping URSULA behind on the sofa.

Lights fade.

End of Act One.

ACT TWO

URSULA *is sleeping on the sofa and slowly comes round as the rest file in.*

URSULA. Was it nice?

IRENE. Not as nice as I remember.

BREDA *pours herself a drink.*

BREDA. It looks better now.

CLARE. Proud of yourself, are you?

BREDA. She insisted on inspecting the garden.

MARIE. You didn't have to follow me.

CLARE. Caught like a pair of rabbits in the headlights.

MARIE *pours a drink for herself and* IRENE. CLARE *pours herself an orange juice but gets distracted and turns away momentarily.* MARIE *seizes this opportunity to sneak a vodka into her drink.*

MARIE. How was I supposed to know the place would light up like football pitch? (*Nudging* BREDA.) See?

BREDA. Don't blame me, it's your fault.

MARIE. Mine? I didn't lob the statue through her window.

BREDA. You're the one always telling me I should stick up for myself.

MARIE. Stick up for yourself, I said, not turn yourself into a vandal.

BREDA. They deserved it. If he thinks he's selling my house to fund fucking Southfork he's another thing coming.

CLARE. Quit it, the pair of you.

CLARE *knocks back a gulp, and then spits it back out into the glass.*

Mam!

MARIE. It'll do you no harm.

CLARE. It's not me I'm worried about.

MARIE. Pardon?

CLARE. Nothing.

MARIE. Back up there now, are you saying what I think you're saying?

CLARE. I'm not saying anything.

IRENE. What's she not saying?

MARIE. She's pregnant.

CLARE. Mam!

They cheer and whoop.

This is why I didn't want to say anything.

IRENE. Group hug.

CLARE. No!

They all stop in their tracks, arms outstretched.

I've been down this road before… so there'll be no talk or excitement until I'm holding this baby in my arms.

MARIE. Ah, Clare –

CLARE. Don't even – I'm so ashamed of you right now I can't even look at you.

MARIE *shuts up and sits on the sofa but can't get comfortable. She moves the cushion a few times until she eventually finds the half-eaten box of Ferrero Rocher.*

MARIE. I didn't see these on your diet sheet.

MARIE *offers the chocolates around, deliberately skipping* BREDA.

Irene? Ursula?

URSULA *shakes her head.*

IRENE. You should try and eat something, Ursula, for soakage.

> BREDA *hobbles across to get a chocolate but* MARIE
> *moves the box out of her way at the last minute.* BREDA
> *hobbles back to her chair.* IRENE *steals a Ferrero and*
> *signals for* BREDA *to take the acupuncture needle out of her*
> *ear.* BREDA *hands the needle to* IRENE *and* IRENE *hands*
> *her a sweet in return.* MARIE *notices the exchange.*

> It's only the one.

MARIE *counts how many are missing.*

MARIE. No, there's one, two, three, four, five missing.

> *Pointing to* BREDA*'s mouth.*

> That'll be six.

URSULA *reaches for the cake tin.*

IRENE. What are you doing?

URSULA. Having some cake… for soakage.

IRENE. Don't ruin your diet.

MARIE. Especially on that.

URSULA. I am allowed to eat… sometimes.

> URSULA *chows down on a big lump of cake. The others*
> *munch on their Ferreros while waiting for the taste to hit*
> URSULA.

> You'll have another bit?

ALL. No thanks… / It's too rich for me…

> *The taste finally hits* URSULA. *She retches into a napkin*
> *and drains the remainder of her drink to wash away the*
> *taste.*

BREDA. You can't beat Max for the sweet stuff.

> URSULA *grabs the cake and slams it into the bin.*

MARIE. Don't worry, Ursula, you can't be good at everything.

> URSULA *bursts into tears.*

BREDA. Don't let Marie upset you.

CLARE. Mam.

IRENE. That's just her way, love.

MARIE. I didn't do ah'in on her.

IRENE. It wasn't that bad, it looked lovely.

URSULA. But it tasted shite, bit of a metaphor for life really.

IRENE. Is there something else?

BREDA. Is it Max, are you's fighting?

   URSULA *nods, crying.*

MARIE. Get her another drink, Clare.

IRENE. Maybe you should go in and talk to him, Ursula.

URSULA. I will slit his throat if I talk to him right now.

IRENE. Nothing wrong with a good row; it clears the air.

   CLARE *pours her another drink but* URSULA *knocks it back before she gets a chance to add a mixer.*

URSULA. Hit me baby one more time.

   CLARE *refills the glass.* URSULA *throws it back again.*

MARIE. It must be bad.

IRENE. Sure, isn't the best part of fighting the making up.

URSULA. There'll be none of that this time around.

IRENE. You say that now –

URSULA. I have chlamydia.

   They are silent.

IRENE. I have that.

URSULA. You do?

IRENE. Yeah, you know what my downfall is? Sausage. I love them, especially Superquinn ones, worst thing for your heart though.

MARIE. Sausage?

IRENE. Well, pork products in general, they're very fatty.

CLARE. Are you talking about your cholesterol, Irene?

IRENE. Yeah, seven point nine it is.

CLARE. Ursula has chlamydia, the infection, you know, down there…

IRENE. Oh… I don't have that.

MARIE. You weren't using public toilets or anything were you, Ursula?

URSULA. He's cheating on me.

BREDA. The bastard.

URSULA (*refers to her eye*). And this is how I found out.

BREDA. Surely the eye is unrelated?

URSULA. You'd think, wouldn't you?

They're all a bit confused.

My head was in the vicinity.

Collective wince.

MARIE. Oh, Jesus help you.

BREDA. They're not made like us, Ursula, if they're hungry they'll just go and eat in another restaurant, do you get me?

URSULA. Oh yeah, dickhead's been going out for lunch every day – with the office temp. He's been working through his tea breaks and taking an hour and a half for lunch.

BREDA. What did you say to that?

URSULA. 'An hour and a half?' I said, 'What did you do for the other hour twenty-five?' You know, I always said if Max ever did anything like this he'd be so quick out on his arse he wouldn't know what hit him. But now here I am, three kids later, what do I do?

BREDA. Poison the fucker.

MARIE. You could bake him a cake.

URSULA. You know what the worst thing is? He asked me what I'd been up to. Me, who wakes up every morning so exhausted it feels like I've been run over.

BREDA. He did not.

URSULA. I threw my Nicholas Mosse vase at him – it's alright, I'm gone off it.

BREDA. A gorgeous-looking girl like you… what's he looking for?

URSULA. My world's been turned upside down.

MARIE. You poor thing.

URSULA. I didn't even suspect.

IRENE. You trusted him, Ursula, don't beat yourself up for that.

BREDA. Sickening… and when it happens… Jaysus, you think you'll never survive.

MARIE. Had you been getting on okay?

URSULA. Fine… or so I thought.

IRENE. How's your hot press?

URSULA. Pardon?

IRENE. Your hot press? Is it a mess, tidy, what's it like?

URSULA. Tidy, I suppose.

IRENE. Hmm…

URSULA. What does hmm… mean?

IRENE. You've three kids, a job and a tidy hot press? Things haven't been going too well in that department, have they?

CLARE. You can tell that from a hot press?

IRENE. Frustrated folding I used to call it. When my second husband, Bobby, was alive, I'd keep an eye on it and if it was too neat, I'd mess it up on purpose and pounce on him that night.

BREDA. Hardly, Irene, how do you think she caught the other thing?

URSULA. She's right, we haven't… (*Refers to eye*.) this was for his fortieth.

MARIE. Close your ears, Clare.

CLARE *puts her hand over her ears*.

I know it's exhausting with small kids, Ursula, but it's important to keep these things alive. Bernard and I still take the Micra down to Dollymount Strand the odd night.

CLARE. Mam!

MARIE. I told you to cover your ears.

URSULA. So it's my fault, is that what you're saying?

MARIE. Ah now.

IRENE. Maybe yis could try talking to someone.

URSULA. I'm not getting the blame for this. You know they'll throw it back on me, that I brought it on myself, that I should be dressing like a French maid and trying out all the new sex tips I read in *Cosmo*, well, there's no more room on my to-do list, I'm knackered.

BREDA. I hear you.

IRENE. You could do with a holiday.

URSULA. You know what I could do with? Someone to help me out, maybe I'll get myself a stupid fucking wife.

BREDA. He'd love that, wouldn't he?

IRENE. Love is like a muscle, you have to keep exercising it.

MARIE. Do you like exercising love muscles, Redback?

IRENE. I do.

CLARE. Mam, stop that.

URSULA. Don't leave me drinking on my own.

Everyone takes a large gulp in sympathy.

Do you think I've let myself go?

BREDA. None of that rubbish talk, you always look gorgeous.

URSULA. I'm not the same, though, am I?

MARIE. We're all getting older, Ursula, and if it's any consolation your Max is ageing fair worse than you. Well, it's true, he's only gone forty, isn't he?

URSULA. Maybe I'll start getting Botox again.

MARIE. For what like?

URSULA. To fill in the cracks on my face. I tried it before, you know, but Jake kept asking me why I stopped blinking.

IRENE. Does Botox stop you blinking?

URSULA. It can leave you looking a bit stunned; I knew where he was coming from.

IRENE. How long ago was that, Ursula?

URSULA. I stopped when I was pregnant on Ciara...

IRENE. That's what that was; I thought your Bell's palsy had come back.

MARIE. Don't, you'll start with a tweak here and a tweak there and before you know it you'll be like that Cat Lady. Sure, look at Kenny Rogers.

URSULA. What about Kenny Rogers?

MARIE. Have you not seen Kenny Rogers? He looks like he escaped from a fire.

IRENE. And he was gorgeous.

MARIE. He was; a fine thing.

BREDA. Sure, Halle Berry's husband cheated on her and she's fabulous looking.

MARIE. There's feck-all hope for the rest of us if Halle Berry can't hold on to her husband.

BREDA. Seemingly he was addicted to sex, he was with loads of different women on her.

IRENE. My third husband, Shay, was addicted to sex, did he teach me a thing or two in the bedroom.

MARIE. I always thought he looked a bit like Tom Selleck.

IRENE. I always thought that too.

CLARE. When you say addicted now?

IRENE. Sometimes two or three times a day. If he wasn't on me, he was on the internet, had me knackered.

CLARE. When he died, you weren't in the middle of...?

IRENE. Oh God no, he was out jogging when he had the heart attack.

CLARE. That's awful.

IRENE. It was.

MARIE. So was that moustache.

BREDA. Have you seen this one he's with, Ursula?

URSULA. We've met, I recommended her for the temping job in his office.

BREDA. Fucking typical.

URSULA. We bumped into her at the St Patrick's Day Parade, she was with her friends wearing a leprechaun hat and a green mini-skirt... she can't be far off thirty and the big arse on her – no offence, Breda. The kids were freezing, Jake was on Max's shoulders, I had Ciara in a sling and Aaron was crying because I couldn't lift him up. She tots over and starts prancing about with Aaron, everyone thought it was hilarious. I wanted to kill her. On the way home, I gave out to Max for flirting with her. He laughed, like it was the most ridiculous thing in the world but I'd planted the seed, before that he didn't think he stood a chance.

MARIE. Do you think he's in love with her?

URSULA. He said he's isn't and can't understand why that doesn't make me feel any better.

MARIE. A young girl like her won't want him full time, Ursula, too much baggage.

URSULA. I don't know whether I want him either.

BREDA. You say that now.

IRENE. Has Max always been a bit of a Mickey Dazzler?

URSULA. Pardon?

IRENE. I meant it as a compliment, he's very attractive.

MARIE. Do you think?

IRENE. Oh yeah, very distinguished.

MARIE. I would've always thought Ursula was a bit of out his league and I'm not just saying that now.

URSULA. Thanks, Marie.

MARIE. I'd say his big fat w–

CLARE. Mam!

MARIE. – wallet helped.

URSULA. He doesn't even have that any more, we're broke. We've had to cut so many corners, I've even started taking the bus, anybody is allowed on the bus. One time this guy sat beside me reeking of cigarettes – I saw him nip it at the stop. Max wouldn't be caught dead on public transport. He'd better not be spending any of my hard-earned cash on her.

BREDA. Part and parcel, Ursula.

IRENE. Not for a lunchtime diddle… I'd say the most he's doing is stopping at the petrol station afterwards and getting her a coffee and a sandwich.

MARIE. Or a Big Mac Meal at the drive-thru that's what we [do]…

BREDA. You keep your running-away money… don't be a thick like me.

URSULA. We're in negative equity.

MARIE. You've a big Jeep sitting outside your door.

URSULA. I need my car, Marie.

MARIE. Sell it and get yourself a little Punto or something.

URSULA. I said we were broke, not destitute. Who knew I could be this thin and so unhappy?

BREDA. It's not fair how the men get to start over while the women are left to rot.

MARIE. Tommy's hardly love's young dream with the hair starting here and sweeping all the way over to here.

IRENE. I always liked Tommy's hair, very Donald Trump.

BREDA. Men my age are chasing girls Clare's age, even Ursula's too old for them.

URSULA. Thanks.

BREDA. You might as well be invisible.

MARIE. Not all of them, Breda.

BREDA. Irene, am I right? Who have you been with since Shay? See? And it's not from her lack of trying.

MARIE. At least she is trying.

BREDA. Don't start.

MARIE. You have to get out there.

BREDA. We'll bring you down to the ballroom-of-no-chance, see how you like it.

MARIE. I'll go with you if you want me to.

BREDA. Bernard would love that, wouldn't he?

MARIE. Bernard doesn't rule me, Breda… he doesn't.

BREDA. They're only ever looking for one thing in those places.

MARIE. To get over one you have to get under another.

URSULA. Seems to be how it works all right.

BREDA. Don't mind that bastard, Ursula.

MARIE. What did that Tommy bastard say to you earlier?

BREDA. I don't know, I wasn't listening to him.

MARIE. He must have said something to set you off…

BREDA. He wants the car.

CLARE. And then Breda told him she was changing the locks.

BREDA. That was a private conversation.

CLARE. There was nothing private about that conversation.

BREDA. He said he was coming for the car and to collect his belongings. I told him I didn't want him in here, taking things.

IRENE. They're only things.

BREDA. I said that from hereon in, we'd be talking through our solicitors.

CLARE. I bet you will.

IRENE *picks a golf club out of the bag to make her point.*

IRENE. They're only things, they don't mean anything.

MARIE. He could have you up for criminal damage.

BREDA. He can get in fucking line.

MARIE. What are you talking about?

BREDA. Nothing.

IRENE. What use is a golf club to you?

BREDA *takes the golf club from her and beats it off the back of the sofa until it is bent.*

BREDA. It's of absolutely no use to me or to anyone else for that matter...

BREDA *hands the club back to* IRENE. *She then picks up some scissors from her stationery table and, taking a garment from one of the black bags, begins to cut the arm off one of Tommy's shirts.* IRENE *approaches to stop her.*

IRENE. Breda –

BREDA *waves the scissors threateningly,* IRENE *backs away.*

BREDA. I might as well be hung for a sheep as a lamb.

MARIE. Is it wrong that I'm a bit impressed?

CLARE. You've created a monster.

IRENE. This can't keep going on.

MARIE. She should've left him years ago... you should've, they've done nothing but make each other miserable.

BREDA. It wasn't all bad.

MARIE. It wasn't all good either.

BREDA. You're hardly an ambassador for Accord.

IRENE. Girls.

MARIE. Keep out of this, Redback.

BREDA. Stop calling her Redback.

MARIE. I'll call her what I like.

BREDA. It's offensive.

MARIE. How?

BREDA. You know well what I mean.

> CLARE *steps in between them, carefully removing the scissors from* BREDA.

CLARE. Okay, let's take the stress out of this situation. Mam! Breda, tapping technique – tap under the eye…

> MARIE *and* BREDA *reluctantly copy* CLARE. *Their tapping gets harder as the sequence progresses.*

MARIE. Sunburn's hardly offensive.

CLARE. Collarbone…

BREDA. Unbelievable.

CLARE. Back of your hand…

MARIE. Sense of humour dot com, download.

CLARE. Close your eyes…

BREDA. It's Croatian for donkey.

CLARE. Open…

MARIE. Yeah right.

CLARE. Look left…

> MARIE *looks right.*

BREDA. Ask Bernard.

CLARE. Look right…

> MARIE *looks left and meets* BREDA*'s stare.*

IRENE. It's Australian actually, for the Black Widow Spider...
I looked it up on Wikipedia.

CLARE. Count!

CLARE, BREDA *and* MARIE. One, two, three, four, five!

CLARE takes a deep cleansing breath.

CLARE. How do we feel, any better?

MARIE. Bitch!

BREDA. I'm the bitch?

MARIE. You knew it meant something else and never said
a word.

BREDA. I didn't know it meant that.

MARIE. Bernard's been calling you Redback for years, to your
face. I'll kill him.

IRENE. He probably didn't know the real meaning, Marie.

BREDA. Oh, he knew.

CLARE. And you didn't?

BREDA. Your father swore blind to me it was Croatian for
donkey.

CLARE. Croatian for donkey isn't exactly a compliment either.

BREDA. Keep out of this, Clare.

MARIE. Don't you speak to my daughter like that.

URSULA. If I wanted a row, I would've stayed at home!

MARIE. You need to snap out of this –

CLARE. Shush, Mam!

MARIE. – Don't fucking shush me, Clare – no wonder she's
depressed, Jaysus, I'm depressed just looking at her.

CLARE. I'm sure if it was that easy, Breda would've done it by
now. If you like I could try unblocking your chakras, Breda.

MARIE. I thought if he ever left it'd be for the best but since
he's gone it's worse you're getting.

BREDA. I'm very sorry if all this has been an inconvenience to you, Marie.

MARIE. I understand you're hurt but you can't keep carrying on like this, you have to get –

BREDA. Get over it?

MARIE. Yeah.

BREDA. Just like that? Is that what you said to Bernard? Get over yourself, Bernard, it's no biggie. And did he, Marie, did he just get over it?

MARIE, *embarrassed, looks at* CLARE.

No, he still doesn't trust you as far as he could throw you, ferries you everywhere, so he knows exactly where you are at all times.

MARIE. Ring your daddy, tell him we'll be leaving early.

BREDA. See, we're not that different, are we?

MARIE. Tommy doesn't want you, Breda, never did.

BREDA. Get out.

MARIE. I won't be in a hurry back.

BREDA. You were never invited around in the first place.

MARIE. We'll see how well you do now, without someone breathing down your neck.

CLARE (*on phone*). Hi, we're ready to go –

BREDA. Did I ever ask for your help?

MARIE. God knows you need it.

BREDA. Nobody asks for your help, nobody ever asks for your help. Always bleedin' on at me, get up, Breda, get out, Breda, clean up this house, Breda.

MARIE. State of the place.

BREDA. That's my business, this is my house.

MARIE. In future I won't bother my arse, would that suit you better?

BREDA. Yeah it would.

CLARE (*on phone*). As soon as you can, Dad, thanks.

MARIE. Good, cos I'm tired of it, Breda, and I'm tired of you.

BREDA. Park your cross on the way out.

MARIE *is about to exit*.

CLARE. Where are you going?

MARIE. I am not waiting here.

CLARE. Mam, it's freezing out there.

BREDA. You're more than welcome to stay here in the warmth, Clare.

MARIE. You'd be as warm outside.

CLARE. Can we not wait in the hall or something?

MARIE. Are you coming?

CLARE *hesitates*.

CLARE. I'll follow you out.

MARIE. Slither.

MARIE *exits*.

Silence.

IRENE *farts*.

IRENE. Oh, excuse me, that's the fat Coke…

URSULA *retches*.

It slipped out, the pair of them have me all upset, I apologise, Ursula, breathe through your mouth.

CLARE. Is she all right?

BREDA. I don't know, I've never seen her put them away like this before.

CLARE. She's not putting them anywhere; look at the state of her.

URSULA. Www… ww…

URSULA *is choking out the word 'water' but they can't understand her.*

CLARE. What's she saying?

BREDA. Baby-sign it.

URSULA *makes the baby sign for water.*

Water, she wants water.

CLARE *rushes to get water but* URSULA *pushes her out of the way and bolts to the sink to throw up.* CLARE *and* IRENE *hold back her hair while she garbles down the sink.*

URSULA. When Max and I started dating, he couldn't fart in front of me, would die of embarrassment if something escaped. Then he relaxed, he got so relaxed he started muting the television to make sure I could hear every last one of them, thought it was hilarious. About a month ago he stopped warning me, walked into the room, dropped the bomb and walked out again – like a terrorist. And now, I'm so sorry I let him away with it, farting like that on me.

IRENE. That cake really didn't agree with you, sure it didn't?

URSULA. He said he was flattered, when he was with her he didn't feel like such a failure. What am I going to do about this temp whore?

IRENE. Our Ringo got that… the poor oul mutt.

CLARE. What are you talking about, Irene?

IRENE. Dis-temp-er, is that what your doggy has, Ursula?

URSULA. I'd say she's susceptible to it alright.

IRENE. I still don't think they've found a cure.

MARIE *enters, carrying a car bumper. She throws it on the floor.*

MARIE. I found out what that rattle is on your car, Breda.

CLARE. Where did you get that?

MARIE. In the garage.

BREDA. You've no business being in my garage.

MARIE. I was cold and it was warmer than waiting in here.

BREDA. It looks worse than it is, I'd a scrape.

MARIE. You were lucky to walk away from it, her car's wrecked.

IRENE. What happened to it?

BREDA. I'd a little accident.

MARIE. It looks like she was out joyriding.

BREDA. You're the one in to joyriding, not me.

MARIE. It was you, wasn't it?

BREDA. What are you talking about?

MARIE. Catherine Brady said the car that caused the power cuts left the scene.

BREDA. The Gospel According to Catherine and what else did she say?

MARIE. That was as far as she got because didn't Daisy interrupt us saying the queue was as far back as the deli – which was a lie, by the way, it was only as far back as the cereals.

BREDA. So I had an accident, lost control and hit the pole... look at the weather out there, it could've happened to anyone.

Silence.

URSULA. Did I ruin the party?

IRENE. Of course not, love.

MARIE. Breda did that all by herself.

BREDA. I thought you'd gone.

MARIE. I did, I am... I'm going.

CLARE. Come on, Ursula, we'll bring you home.

IRENE *puts* URSULA*'s sunglasses on her while* CLARE *drags her to her feet.*

Are you coming with us?

IRENE. I'll hang on for a while, get a taxi.

MARIE. Come with us, we're going the chipper.

URSULA *immediately brightens*.

URSULA. Can I come?

CLARE. We're not.

MARIE. We are.

CLARE. I'm not eating anything deep-fried –

URSULA. I've never eaten chips out of a bag.

IRENE. I'll get a taxi, give us a love.

IRENE *grabs all three into her embrace*.

MARIE. Get off me, Rrr… Irene.

IRENE. Safe home.

BREDA. Clare, you forgot your lids.

CLARE *reaches out for the lids while still trying to hold URSULA up and keep a hold of MARIE*.

CLARE. Thanks again, Breda.

BREDA. You're welcome. (*Whispers*.) I'm delighted for you.

MARIE. Ah, you're great, so you are…

CLARE. Mam, stop that.

MARIE. Stupid bleedin' present…

BREDA. Yours aren't much better.

CLARE. She didn't mean that, Breda.

MARIE. Don't you go apologising for me.

BREDA *pulls out a matching saucepan from the cupboard*.

BREDA. Here, I only had enough for one.

CLARE. You hang on to it if you want it, Breda… I'll save up for mine.

BREDA. Take it.

MARIE. What were you keeping it for?

BREDA. To have.

MARIE. 'Sake.

CLARE. Come on, Tyson.

> CLARE *takes the saucepan and leads* MARIE *and* URSULA *out the door.*

URSULA. I did ruin the party, I'm so embarrassed.

MARIE. Don't start crying again, Ursula, you're nearly home.

> BREDA *holds the door open for* MARIE.

BREDA. Goodnight, Marie.

MARIE. Some baby-sign for you, Breda.

> MARIE *sticks her two fingers up at* BREDA. BREDA *slams the door behind them.*

IRENE. It was great getting everyone together, wasn't it?

BREDA. Brillo.

> BREDA *reaches for the bottle,* IRENE *gets there first.*

IRENE. I'll think we'll have tea. (*Rubbing her stomach.*) Have you any green tea, Breda?

BREDA. Only brown, Irene.

IRENE. Brown's lovely.

BREDA. I'm having one more for the ditch.

> BREDA *rescues the vodka bottle.* IRENE *takes a cup out of the press.*

IRENE. 'World's Best Boss'… gas.

BREDA. That's Mary Ellen's.

IRENE. Was she throwing it out?

BREDA.… Yeah.

> IRENE *sticks on the kettle, it short-circuits with a loud bang.*

Use the microwave.

IRENE *puts the cup of water in the microwave, when she opens the fridge door for milk, the door falls off its hinges and the contents spill all over the floor. The panel falls off the utensil drawer. The microwave pings.* IRENE *attempts to clear up the mess.*

Leave it.

IRENE. No use crying over spilt milk… do you hear me?… spilt milk…

BREDA. I said leave it.

IRENE *joins* BREDA *and takes out her phone.*

IRENE. I'll ring a taxi. It's knocked itself off again. Will you look up my pin? I've no glasses with me.

IRENE *fishes out an address book from her handbag and passes it to* BREDA.

BREDA. What's it under?

IRENE. Mr Pin.

BREDA. Mr Alarm, Mr Banks? If anyone stole your bag you'd be cleared out.

IRENE. The amount of numbers you need these days – do I look like Rain Man to you?

BREDA. One, two, three, four.

IRENE. Sorry… I forgot Caroline changed it for me. Now here I have it… ah, now here, I don't, not yet.

BREDA. Ah here.

BREDA *takes the phone and punches in the pin.*

IRENE. Bring up Cab-co for me there.

BREDA. Use the house phone.

IRENE. I don't know the number.

BREDA. Here, it's ringing.

BREDA *hands her back the phone.*

IRENE. Can you send a taxi to 24 St Gabriel's Road, please? It is, how are you, Janice? Is Danny on?

BREDA. Oh Danny boy… the pipes, the pipes are calling…

IRENE *tries to shut* BREDA *up.*

IRENE. He is… great… no I don't mind waiting, thanks.

BREDA. I don't know where you get your energy.

IRENE. I'm doing no such thing… that's the problem.

BREDA. To be even thinking about it, I wouldn't be able, not at this stage of my life.

IRENE. I still think about it.

BREDA. Believe me, the longer you leave it, the less you'll care.

IRENE. I miss the companionship most of all.

BREDA. Is that what the kids are calling it nowadays? You must still miss Bobby all the same.

IRENE. No one ever came close to filling his shoes.

BREDA. It was nice to hear you talking about him, you rarely mention him these days.

IRENE. People got tired of listening –

BREDA. I didn't –

IRENE. – maybe I'd gotten to the stage where it was easier not to, I was very angry about the whole thing.

BREDA. I thought you were just quiet in yourself.

IRENE. I had a face like a smacked bum for a good few years. It's no joke carrying it around, sure it isn't?

BREDA. Is that how I come across? Because I don't feel that way inside.

IRENE. Have you spoken to Colm at all?

BREDA. No.

IRENE. You should go and see him.

BREDA. He doesn't want me over there.

IRENE. He's blue in the face asking you over.

BREDA. He says I drive him demented from here.

IRENE. You're his mother, that's your job.

BREDA. I wish he'd just come home.

IRENE. His life is there now.

BREDA. I have these nightmares about him getting mugged, or having an accident and being left for dead. I don't want to lose him.

IRENE. You're not going to lose him.

BREDA. Anything could happen to him over there.

IRENE. Anything could happen to him over here.

BREDA. I thought you of all people would understand.

IRENE. I do.

Pause.

BREDA. Funny how life ends up, isn't it? Even 'Teresa the Tramp' feels sorry for me.

IRENE. Why, what did she say to you?

BREDA. It wasn't what she said, it was the way she looked at me. When Tommy caught us in the garden, he was raging, but then she called out and he was right there by her side, so obedient; he was never like that with me. When she turned around to close over the porch door, she looked at me with such… pity. Caught sight of my reflection in the glass, saw myself then, how she sees me, he sees me… pathetic, fat – (*Continues.*)

IRENE. Don't talk like that

BREDA. – something in me snapped. I don't want handies (*Jazz hands.*) fucking sympathy.

IRENE. I know things are tough –

BREDA. I'm not even going to have a job at the end of the month.

IRENE. You'll pick something up.

BREDA. Where? I'm finished working, Irene.

IRENE. If Marie can land herself a job, there's hope for us all. Ursula will help, do up your CV, you've great references.

BREDA. They never even asked me to interview, sent me on a course instead: preparing for retirement. Three days with some child asking me about my 'next chapter'. I sat around the table in that canteen, nodding my head in agreement when everyone was talking about getting rid of the dead wood. Never thought for a minute they were talking about me.

IRENE. I'm so sorry, Breda.

BREDA. That Mary Ellen bitch has had it in for me since day one.

IRENE. If you really feel you've been treated unfairly, you need to get yourself another meeting.

BREDA. There's no point, she's stitched me up good and proper. I made a couple of little mistakes, very minor now, but wasn't she keeping a note of it all in her little bold book. Like how are you supposed to know you've made a mistake unless someone tells you?

IRENE. You're not a mind-reader.

BREDA. No I'm not, thank you.

Pause.

It's so quiet here, there was a time when I used to pray for five minutes' peace. Do you remember that? Kids traipsing in and out, anything that could make a noise was on, the place lit up like a Christmas tree. Walk up the road now... dread seeing the dark house, blare the TV all night long but I can still hear the silence lingering in the background. I never cared what Tommy did outside of here; another bit of noise was all I needed. I know what you're thinking –

IRENE. I wasn't thinking anything at all.

BREDA. We share the same history, he remembers who I used to be.

IRENE. You know what the worst time for me was, about six months or so after Bobby died, when everyone else had moved on and it was only starting to sink in for me. I used to have these dreams that we were out walking with Ringo. Bobby always held my hand, not for romance now, it was so he could drag me along, I drove him mad, looking all around, stopping all the time. Somewhere along the route I'd cop I was dreaming and I'd lie there in darkness trying to hold on to where we were. When I opened my eyes the pain would hit me so hard, I thought I was going to suffocate in the bed. A few times when I was out driving, I thought, I could just keep going, straight into that wall and nobody would ever know... but then I thought of Caroline, she'd know, or be forever wondering, tormenting herself night after night thinking there was something she could have done and how would I explain beyond the grave, that it was my own pain I was trying to end and that I didn't mean to pass it on to her. I'm not going to sit here and tell you it gets easier but the thing about grief, it catches up on you, waits patiently until you're at your lowest, then pounces and there's nothing you can do, you have to let the bugger beat you and hope the next time it strikes it'll be a little less severe.

BREDA. Jaysus, Irene.

IRENE. Sometimes it's more exhausting trying to avoid it.

BREDA. I should be ashamed of myself, shouldn't I? Look at the way you've coped after everything life has thrown at you.

IRENE. Death can sometimes be the kindest way to lose somebody, at least I got nice funerals. I never thought I'd find love again after John but I did, and like, I'm sorry he died an' all but if he hadn't, I never would've met Bobby, Bobby turned out to be the big love of my life. At least John went quick but watching Bobby die like that... Caroline was fifteen, Stephen only four. Lucky for Shay I met him when I was fifty so I was done with the baby thing but he went and died anyway. I was getting wise by then; I hadn't got too attached to him.

BREDA. You know there's more chance of us dying in a plane crash than meeting someone at our age.

IRENE. That's not true because you won't even get on a plane, Breda.

BREDA. When did you know you'd moved on?

IRENE. I don't think I ever moved on.

BREDA. You married Shay a year after Bobby died.

IRENE. I know and I still don't think my kids have forgiven me for it. Tried to fool myself into thinking Bobby had sent Shay along to look after me but who was I kidding? I would've taken Hitler into my bed to feel a warm body next to mine. God forgive me speaking ill of the dead… but Shay was an awful gobshite.

BREDA. Oh, he was.

IRENE. We never would've lasted. I kept expecting Bobby to march through the door…

BREDA. Do you think you'll ever marry again?

IRENE. I hope to but if I don't I don't, I wouldn't want another death on my conscience.

Taxi beeps.

I'll tell him to come back.

BREDA. No, go on.

IRENE. I'll hang on.

BREDA. I'll go to bed for once, I'm knackered. Here, take this with you, you might need a little nightcap.

BREDA *hands her the bottle of Bacardi.* IRENE *stalls.*

Will you go on.

IRENE *picks up the earring and hands it to* BREDA.

IRENE. Don't lose that earring now, new day tomorrow. I'll drop into you on the way home from work, give us a love.

They hug.

BREDA. Thanks.

IRENE. For what?

BREDA. Being a pal, I don't deserve you.

IRENE. You deserve all the nice things in the world, that was my birthday wish for you.

Taxi beeps again.

BREDA. You better hurry up, you haven't snogged him yet, he'll have the meter running.

IRENE. I'm gone.

> IRENE *exits.* BREDA *refills her glass and then reaches into her handbag, taking out a couple of bags from different chemists. She sips her drink while contemplating the pill bottles. The phone rings.*

BREDA. Colm love, how are you? Not at all, I'm still up, the girls were here. Irene, Ursula from next door and Marie brought her Clare over – she looks great, still talking about you, son, I don't think she ever really got over you. How's Alice? Oh, I forgot you were going away. No, you did tell me – did I leave lots of messages? Sorry about that. So? Ah, I'm delighted for you. Go on then. Hi ye, Alice… congratulations, I'll have to dust off my hat. Oh, I will this time… promise. Okay, bye, bye, pet. Hi ye. Yeah, as if I'm going to fly over there on my own, Colm… Of course I… (*Pause.*) Are you sure? (*Trying to keep it together.*) Well, I won't land on you; I'll stay in a hotel or something. I'll get Ursula on the internet for me tomorrow and let you know. There's no need for you to take care of anything, Colm… Colm… you're very good. Go on then, goodnight. Colm… I love you, I'm so happy for you, son – I only had two vodkas! I'll talk to you tomorrow. Goodnight.

> *Looking around at the mess, she drains the last of her drink, picks up her earring, examines it and eventually sticks it back in her ear. Heading towards the stairs, she stops to rescue her dance shoes from the mess and nestles them under the coat rack. She switches off the living-room light and exits. As lights fade, Al Green's version of 'How Do You Mend a Broken Heart?' plays.*

The End.

A Nick Hern Book

Shush first published in Great Britain in 2013 as a paperback original by Nick Hern Books Limited, The Glasshouse, 49a Goldhawk Road, London W12 8QP, in association with the Abbey Theatre, Dublin

Shush copyright © 2013 Elaine Murphy

Elaine Murphy has asserted her moral right to be identified as the author of this work

Cover image: ZERO-G.IE (Basia Grzybowska)
Cover design: Ned Hoste, 2H

Typeset by Nick Hern Books, London
Printed and bound in Great Britain by CPI Group (UK) Ltd

A CIP catalogue record for this book is available from the British Library

ISBN 978 1 84842 322 0

CAUTION All rights whatsoever in this play are strictly reserved. Requests to reproduce the text in whole or in part should be addressed to the publisher.

Amateur Performing Rights Applications for performance, including readings and excerpts, by amateurs in the English language throughout the world should be addressed to the Performing Rights Manager, Nick Hern Books, The Glasshouse, 49a Goldhawk Road, London W12 8QP, *tel* +44 (0)20 8749 4953, *e-mail* info@nickhernbooks.co.uk, except as follows:

Australia: Dominie Drama, 8 Cross Street, Brookvale 2100, *fax* (2) 9938 8695, *e-mail* drama@dominie.com.au

New Zealand: Play Bureau, PO Box 420, New Plymouth, *fax* (6) 753 2150, *e-mail* play.bureau.nz@xtra.co.nz

South Africa: DALRO (pty) Ltd, PO Box 31627, 2017 Braamfontein, *tel* (11) 712 8000, fax (11) 403 9094, *e-mail* theatricals@dalro.co.za

United States of America and Canada: Curtis Brown Ltd, see details below.

Professional Performing Rights Application for performance by professionals in any medium and in any language throughout the world should be addressed to Curtis Brown Ltd, Haymarket House, 28-29 Haymarket, London SW1Y 4SP, *tel* +44 (0)20 7393 4400, *fax* +44 (0)20 7393 4401, *e-mail* cb@curtisbrown.co.uk

No performance of any kind may be given unless a licence has been obtained. Applications should be made before rehearsals begin. Publication of this play does not necessarily indicate its availability for amateur performance.

www.nickhernbooks.co.uk

facebook.com/nickhernbooks

twitter.com/nickhernbooks